Turning the world upside down

Illustrations by Tim Benton

kevin mayhew

www.kevinmayhew.com

kevin mayhew

First published in Great Britain in 2017 by Kevin Mayhew Ltd
Buxhall, Stowmarket, Suffolk IP14 3BW
Tel: +44 (0) 1449 737978 Fax: +44 (0) 1449 737834
E-mail: info@kevinmayhew.com

www.kevinmayhew.com

© Copyright 2017 Claire Benton-Evans.

The right of Claire Benton-Evans to be identified as the author of this work has been asserted by her in accordance with the Copyright, Designs and Patents Act 1988.

The publishers wish to thank all those who have given their permission to reproduce copyright material in this publication.

Every effort has been made to trace the owners of copyright material and we hope that no copyright has been infringed. Pardon is sought and apology made if the contrary be the case, and a correction will be made in any reprint of this book.

All rights reserved. No part of this publication may be reproduced, stored in a retrieval system, or transmitted, in any form or by any means, electronic, mechanical, photocopying, recording, or otherwise, without the prior written permission of the publisher.

9 8 7 6 5 4 3 2 1 0

ISBN 978 1 84867 866 8
Catalogue No. 1501534

Cover design by Rob Mortonson
Illustrations by Tim Benton
Edited by Nicki Copeland
Typeset by Justin Minns

Printed and bound in Great Britain

He's Alive!

Escape to Emmaus – there and back again 7
Holey Lord – Thomas investigates 13
Come and have breakfast! – the beach barbecue 19
Up! – the Ascension 25

Daring Disciples

Wind, wildfire and wonderful words – the story of Pentecost 33
Standing up for Jesus – the death of Stephen 39
Total turnaround – Saul becomes a new man 47
Tuck in! – no more food rules 53

Turning the World Upside Down

Angelic escape – Peter busts out of prison 61
Prison break quake – Paul and Silas behind bars 67
From strength to strength – the good news keeps on spreading 73
Shipwreck and snakebite – Paul's adventures 81

Beastly Bonus Story

The end and the beginning – John's jaw-dropping dream 91

ABOUT THE AUTHOR

Claire loves stories and drama but she never once played the Angel Gabriel in a school Nativity play. She studied English at Oxford, where she enjoyed reading lots of very old poems about monsters, battles and God. She gets her best ideas for writing when she's walking her dog and loves living in Scotland because she likes shortbread and mountains. She lives with her husband – a minister – and three children. They all have their own big ideas about Church and they dared her to write **Beastly Bible Stories**.

Details of all Claire's titles can be found on her website at:

www.clairebentonevans.com

www.kevinmayhew.com

ESCAPE TO EMMAUS
There and back again

On the run

'WATCH OUT! SOLDIERS!' The two disciples dodged down a back alley with their hearts thumping like hammers.

'THIS WAY – QUICK!' hissed Cleopas to his friend as the Roman guards marched past, looking for troublemakers. The two terrified disciples slipped away into the shadows. They had been in hiding for three days, ever since the Romans had killed their friend and leader, Jesus. If the Romans caught them, they could end up nailed to a cross, too. It was time to get out of town – **FAST**!

Over walls, through tunnels and under fences, the pair ran like rats through the city's backstreets. By teatime they were out in the open air at last, far beyond the city walls, on a quiet desert road which led to a village called Emmaus. Most people either never knew the place existed or found it hard to remember exactly where it was, and this suited the disciples just fine. Cleopas had relatives in Emmaus, and he and his friend could hide in his cousin's house until all this trouble about Jesus blew over.

A strange meeting

As they walked, they talked about Jesus: 'Do you remember how the soldiers whipped him? Did you hear the crowds shouting? Did you see how long he was hanging on that cross? Did you see how dark it got? Did you feel the earthquake when he died?' Suddenly they heard footsteps behind them – **PANIC**! Had they been followed? Had a spy just heard them mention Jesus? Hardly daring to breathe, they turned around and – **PHEW**! – it was just an ordinary Jewish bloke like them, with dusty feet and a cloth around his face to keep out the sun and sand. He caught up with them.

'So,' the stranger began, 'what's up?'

'What do you mean?' said Cleopas suspiciously.

'Well,' said the stranger, 'what's the news? What are you two talking about?'

'Have you been living in a cave or something? How can you have come from Jerusalem and not *know*?'

'Know what?' said the stranger.

Cleopas sighed. 'You know Jesus? The preacher and teacher who did all those amazing miracles? The one we all thought was God's Son, the Messiah? The one we hoped would save us all? The one our chief priests had **CRUCIFIED** by the Romans three days ago?'

The stranger simply said, 'What about him?'

Cleopas' words began to tumble out. 'What about him?! He's been dead for three days, that's what – we all saw him die – and this morning some of our friends – the women – went to his tomb and he wasn't there! No body! And they said they saw angels! And the angels said that Jesus is **ALIVE**! Some of the others went and checked – and his body really **IS** gone! Now we don't know what to think!'

The stranger shook his head. 'How stupid are you? Don't you see that all this had to happen to the Messiah? First death, then glory! Look – let me explain . . .'

For the next two hours, the stranger talked and the two runaway disciples listened. He explained the Scriptures to them, all the way from Moses and the people of God to the prophecies about the Messiah. Now, all that Bible study may not sound brilliant to you, but the disciples' hearts burned with excitement. It was like hearing all about your favourite book from the person who actually wrote it; it was like listening to the best teacher you've ever had, and suddenly realising that you actually *understand*.

Before they knew it, they found themselves in the tiny village of Emmaus at sunset. They stopped outside the little house where they knew that cool drinks and warm bread would be waiting for them on the table, and they realised how hungry, thirsty and tired they were. They had walked for miles! Now at last they could wash their dusty feet, eat a meal in peace and sleep safely, knowing that they were miles away from Jerusalem and the soldiers. They wondered whether the rest of the disciples were safe and whether Jesus really had come back from the dead. If so, where was he now?

There and back again

At that moment, Cleopas noticed that the stranger was walking off. '**HEY!**' he shouted. 'You don't want to walk all night! Why not come and eat with us?' The stranger nodded, and together the three men went inside.

'**PHEW!**' said Cleopas as he sat down to eat.

'**MMMM!**' said his friend as he smelt the fresh bread.

The stranger took the bread, blessed it and broke it. He said, 'Take this and eat it,' and he smiled a real, crinkly-around-the-eyes smile.

'**WHHAAA– ?!?**' The two disciples gawped as they suddenly recognised him: **IT WAS JESUS!** They turned to each other with their mouths open like landed fish – and when they turned back to look at him, he was gone!

'**IT WAS HIM!**' said one.

'**IT WAS REALLY HIM!**' said the other.

'BUT HOW—? BUT WHEN—? BUT WHAT—?' they gabbled. Then together they both said, '**WE'VE GOT TO TELL THE OTHERS!**'

Did they finish their dinner? No. Did they stop to think? No. Did they wonder whether it was wise to walk a lonely road at night to a city where soldiers were waiting to round them up? I don't think so. They couldn't wait to tell their friends about Jesus, so they just went.

Past the table, through the door and under the night sky, the pair ran like racehorses towards Jerusalem. By midnight they were back in the city, hammering on the locked door of the disciples' hideout. '**HE'S BACK!**' they gasped as the door burst open and they fell into the arms of their astonished friends. '**WE MET HIM! JESUS IS ALIVE!**'

After his Resurrection, Jesus returned to his friends for a short time. This appearance on the road to Emmaus is particularly dramatic because they didn't recognise him for so long! Read on for more visits from Jesus, back from the dead.

You can read this story in Luke 24:13-35.

HOLEY LORD
Thomas investigates

In hiding

'**SSHHH!**' hissed Peter. The disciples shushed. If anyone outside were to hear them arguing about Jesus, they'd be dead men, just like Jesus himself – except that now, three days after his horrible death, some were claiming that he wasn't dead any more! The others couldn't believe it: no wonder they were arguing.

'Now, quiet, everyone!' said Peter. **KER-KLUNK!** He unlocked the heavy door of their hideout. **SKREEEE!** He opened the door a crack and peered out into the dark street. 'OK, coast's clear!' he hissed. 'Thomas, it's your turn – go and find us some bread, and make sure no one follows you back here! Now **GO!**'

Thomas scooted through the door like a frightened cat. **KLUN-KERK!** Peter locked the door again behind him. **PHEW!** For the time being the disciples were safe: safe from all the angry Jews who might report them, and safe from the Romans who were rounding up troublemakers left, right and centre. They turned back to their arguments.

Suddenly – '**IT'S HIM!**' yelled someone. There in the middle of the room was **JESUS**!

'**AARGH!**' screamed someone else, thinking he was a ghost.

'**BUT HOW–? BUT WHEN–? BUT WHAT–?**' the disciples gabbled.

'**PEACE BE WITH YOU!**' said Jesus, and everyone gasped. He sounded just like his old self. Then he held out his hands, and the disciples shuddered to see the red holes in his palms, where the nails had been hammered right through. Jesus pulled open his robe and showed the gash in his side, where the soldiers had poked him with a spear.

'**IT'S REALLY YOU!**' the disciples cheered, then everyone hugged Jesus and one another. Did they remember how they had all run away when the soldiers arrested their friend? Peter can't have forgotten saying not once, but three times, that he didn't even know Jesus. Maybe there was awkwardness mixed with their awe, and sadness mingled with their celebrations.

Over all the noisy excitement, Jesus said again (only louder), '**PEACE BE WITH YOU!**' A hush fell. He said, 'God sent me to do a job. Now I'm sending you. I'm giving you the Holy Spirit and the power to forgive sins!' He took a deep breath and breathed over his disciples, and they felt his warm life touch them. Then, as suddenly as he had come, he was gone.

KNOCK   KNO-KNO-KNO   KNOCK   KNOCK!

The noise at the door made everyone jump, but they recognised the secret knock that meant 'it's one of us' – Thomas was back with the bread. Peter put his finger to his lips and everyone held their breath as **KER-KLUNK!** he unlocked the heavy door of their hideout. **SKREEEE!** He opened the door a crack and pulled Thomas inside. **KLUN-KERK!** Peter locked the door again behind him. Then everyone burst out together: '**WE'VE SEEN HIM! YOU JUST MISSED HIM! YOU WON'T BELIEVE IT!**'

'Who? What?' said Thomas, dropping the bread.

'**JESUS! HE WAS HERE! WE'VE SEEN HIM!**'

Thomas looked at his friends' flushed faces and gleaming eyes and thought they had all gone mad. What a story! Jesus – alive? After the way he died on the cross? Surely not! 'Show me the nail holes in his hands,' he said. 'Let me poke the gash in his side. *Then* I'll believe he's alive.'

Body of evidence

One week later, the disciples were still in hiding and still arguing about Jesus. On one side was everyone who had seen Jesus alive since his death: Mary and Mary who had met him outside his empty tomb, Cleopas and his friend who had met him on the road to Emmaus, and all the others who had hugged him when he had come to them behind locked doors the week before. On the other side was Thomas, who hadn't seen anything and couldn't believe it.

Suddenly – '**IT'S HIM!**' someone yelled. There in the middle of the room was **JESUS**!

'**PEACE BE WITH YOU!**' said Jesus, and everyone smiled – except Thomas, who gawped. Jesus looked straight at Thomas and held out his hands. He showed him the red holes right through his palms and said, 'See these? Put your finger in here!' Then he showed the gash in his side, took Thomas' hand and said, 'Feel this! Put your hand here! You'd better believe it – go on!'

So Thomas peered like a detective at the holes in Jesus' hands. He spied daylight through them and poked his finger into them. Then he scrutinised the spear wound in Jesus' side, fingering the flesh like a surgeon. At last he was convinced. He looked into Jesus' face and gasped, '**MY LORD AND MY GOD!**'

Jesus replied, 'So you believe in me now because you've seen me, is that it? If anyone believes in me *without* having seen me, they're really blessed!'

Poor Thomas has been known as 'doubting Thomas' ever since, but all the disciples were doubters until they actually met Jesus, back from the dead – then they were believers. It is good to know that if we believe in Jesus without seeing him, then we are blessed: he said so himself!

You can read this story in John 20:19-31.

COME AND HAVE BREAKFAST!
The beach barbecue

Flashbacks and fishing

'**COCK-COCK-COCK-A-DOODLE-DOO!**' Simon Peter jumped. He and his friends were back home by the Sea of Galilee, safe from soldiers and search parties, but the cry of a cockerel took him straight back to that terrible night when Jesus was arrested and people kept questioning Peter about him. Again and again in his head, Peter heard himself deny Jesus three times: 'I don't know who you're talking about,' 'I don't even know who you mean,' and – worst of all – '**I DON'T KNOW HIM, ALL RIGHT?!**' And then '**COCK-COCK-COCK-A-DOODLE-DOO!**' just as Jesus had predicted.* And now Jesus was back from the dead, and Peter wished he could turn back time and give three totally different answers.

'**RIGHT!**' Peter leapt to his feet and shook himself, trying to get rid of his shame as a dog shakes off water. 'I'm going fishing!' he declared as he stomped off down to the beach.

* You can read this story in *Bad Friday* in **Beastly Bible Stories 7**.

'Wait for us!' called his friends. 'We're coming too!' Fishing sounded a better plan than hanging around to see when Jesus would turn up again. Besides, it was like the old days: as James and John climbed into their little boat with the others, they remembered how Jesus had first met them there and said, 'Follow me!' And they had, just like that.*

As the sun began to set, Peter and the disciples cast their nets into the water and waited for the fish.

Beach barbecue

If you went sea fishing today, you'd wear special waterproofs, fishing wellies, a life jacket, big gloves and bright orange waders like dayglo dungarees. Simon Peter and the six other disciples went fishing the way professional fishermen did in those days – wearing nothing at all. That's right, STARKERS! Think about it: the weather was hot, the water was warm, and long robes got in the way: with heavy nets to cast and ropes to haul, it made sense to strip off and get stuck in.

So this bare-bottomed bunch of disciples fished all night, but – just like their last fishing trip three years earlier – their nets came up empty every time.

As the dawn sky brightened and they drifted closer to the shore, they noticed a stranger standing on the beach. He called to them, 'You haven't caught anything, have you?'

* You can read this story in *Freaky Fish* in **Beastly Bible Stories 5**.

'**NO!**' they shouted back.

'Try casting your nets on the other side!' he said. **HEEAANGH!** They heaved the empty nets into the boat. **HUURGH-SPLOOOOSH!** They hauled them over the other side. Suddenly – **SSSSWIIIIIP!** The ropes jerked like live eels in their hands. They pulled – **HEAVE!** – and pulled – **HEAVE!** – and pulled – **HEAVE!** – until they could see that their nets were full of flapping, flashing, silver fish.

One of the disciples pointed at the smiling stranger on the beach and yelled, '**IT'S HIM – JESUS!**' Simon Peter leapt to his bare feet. *Is it really him?* he wondered, and he couldn't wait to find out. He wriggled into his robes, threw himself into the sea and doggy-paddled to dry land. The rest of the disciples rowed the boat, dragging their bulging fishing nets behind them.

A delicious smell tickled the disciples' noses as they reached the beach and clumsily climbed back into their clothes. Bread toasting over a charcoal fire – **YUM!** The stranger (was he really Jesus?) said, 'Let's have some of your fish, then!' So Peter hauled the nets out of the boat – **HEAVE!** – and, like good fishermen, they all counted the catch: 153 enormous fish!

The stranger (was he really the Lord?) balanced some of the fish over the fire and said, 'Come and have breakfast!' He took the bread, blessed it and broke it; then he shared out the fish. He said, 'Tuck in! There's enough for

EVERYONE!' The disciples sat down and ate. Mmmm . . . Hot toast with barbecued fish fresh from the sea – delicious! No one dared to say, 'Who are you?' because anyone could see it was Jesus himself.

Last orders

When they had licked their fishy fingers and wiped the last crumbs from their beards, the men around the fire fell silent. Simon Peter couldn't help remembering the last time he had sat by a fire like this, outside the house where Jesus had been a prisoner, and yet again in his head, helplessly, Peter heard himself deny Jesus three times: 'I don't know who you're talking about,' 'I don't even know who you mean,' and – worst of all – '**I DON'T KNOW HIM, ALL RIGHT?!**'

Suddenly Jesus turned to Peter and asked, 'Peter, do you love me?'

'Yes, Lord,' replied Peter. 'You know that I love you.'

'Feed my lambs,' said Jesus. Everyone around the fire remembered that Jesus had described himself as 'the good shepherd'. His people were his flock, and it sounded as though it was Peter's job to look after them now.

Peter nodded, then Jesus said again, 'Peter, do you love me?'

'Yes, Lord,' said Peter for the second time. 'You know that I love you.'

'Look after my flock,' said Jesus.

There was a pause, and then for the third time Jesus asked, 'Peter, do you love me?'

Peter felt ready to cry – how many times would he have to say it? For the third time he said, 'Lord, you know everything – you **KNOW** that I love you.'

Jesus smiled a real, crinkly-around-the-eyes smile and said, 'Feed my sheep.' He looked hard at Peter. 'Follow me.'

Peter gawped like one of the fish on the fire to hear those familiar words again. Then he turned around and looked at the rest of the disciples. 'But what about them?'

Jesus replied, 'Peter, I'm asking **YOU** to **FOLLOW ME**!'

This is the final story of John's Gospel. It shows Peter once again as leader of the disciples, with an important job to do – looking after all Jesus' followers, as Jesus himself did. When Jesus first called Simon 'Peter', he made him head of the Church, and ever since Peter, it has been the Church's job to look after 'the flock' (Jesus' followers) and 'the lost sheep' (everyone else who needs love, care or help).

You can read this story in John chapter 21.

UP!
The Ascension

When?

Do you remember the garden where Jesus was arrested? It was where he said to his friends, 'Can you keep me company?' but they fell asleep and then ran away when the soldiers came.* Now, 40 days later, they were (almost) all back together in the same garden. During those 40 days, they hadn't run out of questions for their resurrected leader. 'So, Lord,' began one disciple, 'about you saving Israel from the Romans – when is that going to happen, exactly?'

'That's up to God,' replied Jesus. 'What I **CAN** promise you is that you'll get the **POWER OF THE HOLY SPIRIT** and you'll be my witnesses here, there and everywhere!' The disciples stared at him as their brains boggled. *Power?* they wondered. *For us? What does that mean?*

Where? Why?

As the disciples gawped at Jesus, something very strange began to happen. At first, they thought he was getting taller – **IMPOSSIBLE!** Then they saw

---

* You can read this story in *Final Feast* in **Beastly Bible Stories 7**.

his feet leave the ground. They watched as he floated **UP, UP, UP** above their heads and high above the crooked olive trees in the garden. '**LORD!**' they shouted. '**WHERE ARE YOU GOING?**' But Jesus simply smiled his real, crinkly-around-the-eyes smile and disappeared into the clouds.

The disciples craned their necks and squinted as they tried to see where Jesus had gone.

'**HEY, YOU!**' said a man's voice. The disciples jumped and looked around. Two men in bright white clothes had appeared from nowhere. '**YES, YOU LOT FROM GALILEE!**' said the first man, like a teacher trying to get his class's attention.

'Why are you staring at the sky?' asked the second stranger. 'Jesus has gone up into heaven, and one day he'll come back to earth in the same way.' With that, the shining strangers disappeared and the disciples looked at each other. *Was that the last time we'll ever see him?* they wondered.

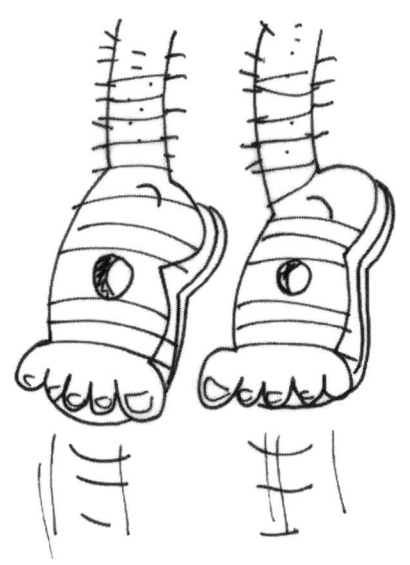

What?

Amazed and confused, the disciples made their way back to Jerusalem together, wondering where in heaven's name Jesus had gone and what on earth they were going to do now. Do you remember who they all were? Here's the line-up:

1. Peter (who used to be Simon) the fisherman
2. Andrew the fisherman, Peter's brother
3. James the fisherman
4. John the fisherman, James' brother (Jesus nicknamed them 'the Thunder Boys')
5. Philip
6. Bartholomew (also known as Nathaneal)
7. Matthew (also known as Levi. He used to be an unpopular tax collector)
8. Thomas (who wanted proof that Jesus really had come back from the dead)
9. James, Alphaeus' son
10. Simon (Jesus nicknamed him 'the Zealot')
11. Thaddeus (also known as Judas, James' son)
12. Er . . . that's it, because of course Judas Iscariot had betrayed Jesus, and no one had seen him since.

So 11 disciples went back to their den, where they were hiding out with Jesus' family and his special friends, including the women who had first seen his empty tomb and spread the good news. The strange story tumbled out: 'He's gone! He just went up and up into the sky! We couldn't see him any more! There were these men – angels, I reckon! They said he'd gone to heaven! His last words were a promise: he said we'd get God's power! "The power of the Holy Spirit," that's what he said!'

Once the tale had been told, retold and picked apart, a silence fell on the small group of believers. 'So what do we do now?' someone asked.

Everyone answered, '**PRAY**!' So they did. They all stayed and prayed together while they waited for whatever God was going to do next.

This final appearance (and disappearance) of Jesus is known as the Ascension. It's an extraordinary story that might remind you of what happened to other holy people, like Elijah.* It was the last time the disciples saw Jesus, but they had lots more work to do for him! Read on to find out what the disciples did next . . .

You can read the story of the Ascension in Acts 1:6-14.

* You can read this story in *On Fire* in **Beastly Bible Stories 1**.

DARING DISCIPLES

WIND, WILDFIRE AND WONDERFUL WORDS
The story of Pentecost

Crowd control

Do you remember the crowds in Jerusalem during the Passover Festival, when Jesus was killed? The place was packed with pilgrims, and there were locals, visitors and tourists everywhere: it was busier than a beach on a bank holiday. Now, 50 days after Passover, it was happening all over again. This time it was the Jewish Harvest Festival,* which the Bible calls Pentecost. As if a massive fishing net had been flung across the Mediterranean from Rome to Saudi Arabia and from Egypt to Iran,** Jewish pilgrims were drawn in to Jerusalem, where they were packed into the local hotels like sardines in a tin. Roman soldiers patrolled the city, on the lookout for any more crowd trouble.

---

* This festival celebrated the wheat harvest, seven weeks or 50 days after Passover. It's called Shavuot (Weeks) in Hebrew and Pentecost (Fiftieth) in Greek.
** Some of these places had different names in those days: Saudi Arabia was called Arabia and a part of Iran was called Parthia.

Fire power

Meanwhile, in a den in the backstreets of the city, Jesus' disciples were still in hiding – just as they had been since Jesus had gone back up to heaven, leaving them with his mysterious promise: 'You'll get the **POWER OF THE HOLY SPIRIT** and you'll be my witnesses here, there and everywhere!' No one really knew what that meant, but there they all were, waiting and praying, praying and waiting, behind locked doors.

Suddenly – **WHOOOOOOOSH! SWOOOOOOOSH!** A wild wind swooped through the house! It threw the disciples' beards in their faces and tossed their hair in their eyes. It whipped up dust tornadoes from the floor and tore blankets off the beds. Behind the locked door and windows, this indoor hurricane filled the whole house! **SWOOO-WOOO-HOOOOOSH! WHOOO-HOOO-SWOOOOOSH!** Each disciple felt the wind buffet him in the face like a bird's beating wing.

'**FIRE!**' shouted Andrew, pointing wildly at his brother. '**YOU'RE ON FIRE!**' He was right – flames were leaping in the air above Peter's head. The disciples looked round in panic and saw fire dancing above everyone's head – but no one was burning or screaming! Instead they felt wonderfully strong as the Holy Spirit poured into them. God's superpower had arrived!

Now the Holy Spirit was in charge, telling the disciples what to say and pushing them out into the crowded streets to say it. '**PRAISE THE LORD!**' they shouted. '**JESUS IS LORD! PRAISE BE TO GOD!**' Or rather, that's what they meant to say – but what came out of their mouths was something like, '**KOH-dah-rah SHOH-kr!**' or '**MAHG-duh lah rahp!**' or '**Ki-reon Yess-oun!**' or '**Louse DAY-oh!**' What were they saying? What was going on? The Holy Spirit knew, and so did the growing crowd of pilgrims who were gathering round to listen. No matter what country they came from, they heard the disciples speaking their language!*

'**AMAZING!**' said one pilgrim from Egypt. 'These blokes are all from Galilee, but I can understand **EVERY WORD!** They're saying that God has brought Jesus back from the dead!'

A visitor from Asia exclaimed, '**HOW IS THIS HAPPENING?!**'

No one was more astonished than the disciples themselves, but a group from Rome jeered, '**HA!** They're just drunk!'

Then Peter stepped forward and shouted, '**LISTEN!** We're **NOT** drunk – anyway, it's first thing in the morning! **NO** – this is the Holy Spirit talking, just as the Lord promised! It's his gift to **EVERYONE** – men,

---

* In modern-day Iran, 'KOH-dah-rah SHOH-kr' is how you say 'Praise the Lord' in Farsi. 'MAHG-duh lah rahp' means the same in Arabic. 'Kireon Yess-oun' is how you say 'Jesus is Lord' in Greek, and 'Louse DAY-oh' is how you say 'Praise be to God' in Latin.

women, children and old people alike! It's all because of **JESUS** – remember **HIM?** You saw his miracles with your own eyes! Then you nailed him to the cross and killed him, but God brought him back from the dead! So **HERE'S HOW IT IS:** God gave you Jesus as your Lord and Messiah, and you crucified him!'

The pilgrims who were packed in around Peter understood every word. A grim silence settled on the crowd as the people realised exactly what they had done. One man called out to the disciples, 'What can we do, brothers?'

Peter, prompted by the Holy Spirit, had his answer ready: 'Say sorry and be baptised in the name of Jesus the Messiah! Ask God to forgive your sins and he'll give you the gift of his Holy Spirit!'

The Church's birthday

At that, the crowd of pilgrims fell over each other in their haste to say sorry. They couldn't wait for God's forgiveness! **SPLOOOSH! SPLOOOSH! SPLOOOSH!** Peter and the disciples spent hours baptising the new believers. That Pentecost was the day the Christian Church was born, and more than 3000 people became its newest members!

When the Festival was over, and those pilgrims went back to Rome, Saudi Arabia, Egypt, Iran and all the Mediterranean countries in between, they took their new faith with them. They told an amazing story about Jesus, the miracle-making Messiah who came back from the dead, and God's superpower, the Holy Spirit. And so the good news (or *gospel*) started to spread here, there and everywhere, just as Jesus had said it should.

The Holy Spirit is the hero of this story, making an entrance as wind and fire before giving the disciples the power to do things they would never have thought possible. Remember, these were the same disciples who had been in hiding since Jesus' death because they were terrified of the Romans: the Holy Spirit sent them out into the crowded streets to shout about Jesus! These were ordinary blokes from Galilee who hadn't passed exams: the Holy Spirit made them speak in all sorts of different languages, so that everyone could understand them! This is how the Christian Church began, and the Holy Spirit was just getting started...

You can read the story of Pentecost in Acts 2:1-41.

STANDING UP FOR JESUS
The death of Stephen

Team Jesus

WOW! The first Christians had never heard anything as exciting as the good news about Jesus. They stayed together and shared everything: their new faith, their food, their prayers and even their possessions! No one was poor or hungry, and they all looked out for each other. But this wasn't a secret club: the good news about Jesus was so amazing that the first Christians just couldn't keep it to themselves . . .

BAM! Peter and John turned up at the Temple. **WOOMF!** They cured a man who'd been crippled since birth. '**WOAH!**' People were amazed.

'**WHAT?**' said Peter. 'Why are you so impressed? **GOD** did this miracle – the same all-powerful God who sent you a Saviour – Jesus the **MESSIAH** – and **YOU KILLED HIM**, but **GOD** brought him **BACK FROM THE DEAD!** Say **SORRY** and be **SAVED**, in the name of Jesus!' **BOOM!** That was Peter, telling it like it is in the Temple.

'**WOW!**' People were astonished, and immediately more than 5000 folk believed in Jesus.

The Opposition

But not everyone was impressed. The chief priests and the scribes (remember them?) were very annoyed to see yet more troublemaking teaching in *their* Temple. They gave the order: '**ARREST THOSE MEN!**' The disciples spent the night in prison.

The next day, the Chief Priest and the scribes questioned Peter and John. 'Who made you do this?'

Peter looked at the powerful men who had sent Jesus to his death and replied, 'It was **JESUS OF NAZARETH**, the **MESSIAH** you killed on the cross! His name is all-powerful, and it's only through him that any of us can be saved from our sins!'

The Chief Priest wondered at the ordinary fishermen who had been friends with that troublemaking teacher. They had all run away: how had they become such brave, bold big-mouths? He stared hard at Peter and John. 'Now listen to me. You are **NEVER** to mention the name of Jesus again, do you hear? Or you'll be in **BIG TROUBLE**.'

But Peter replied, '**GOD**'s the boss of us, not **YOU**! We can't **STOP** talking about Jesus!'

The more miracles they made, the more popular the disciples became. Crowds of sick people followed them everywhere, yelling, '**HELP ME! MAKE ME BETTER! CURE ME! ME! ME!**' Peter rolled up his sleeves and set to work. **WHAP!** He wiped out one man's fever. **POW!** He fixed a woman's broken back. **WHOOSH!** He banished bad spirits. Miracle after miracle! The crowds went wild. Every day, more and more people believed in Jesus and joined the Church.

The priests, the scribes and all the important religious people in the Temple took the disciples to court. The Chief Priest said to Peter and John, 'Didn't I tell you **NEVER** to mention the name of Jesus again? Didn't I say you'd be in **BIG TROUBLE?**'

But Peter replied, 'We do what **GOD** tells us, not **YOU!** **HE** brought **JESUS** back from the dead, after **YOU** killed him on the cross! Jesus is **OUR SAVIOUR**, we are his witnesses and we've got **GOD'S HOLY SPIRIT** on our side!'

'Sir,' whispered a wise old man in the Chief Priest's ear. 'He might be right, you know! If God really is on their side, nothing can stop them – there's no way we can win!'

'**HUMPH!**' said the Chief Priest and glared at the disciples. 'Just **STOP TALKING ABOUT JESUS!**' he warned, then he ordered them to be whipped – **WHAP! WHAP! WHAP! WHAP! WHAP! WHAP!** – and sent them away.

Stone dead

But nothing could stop the disciples: they went on preaching, teaching and healing everywhere they went. One new disciple called Stephen amazed people with miracles and wowed them with wonders – but when he spoke up in the synagogue, his words of wisdom drove his enemies wild. They plotted and planned, and before Stephen knew what had happened, he found himself in court being questioned by the High Priest. 'He's guilty of blasphemy!' Stephen's enemies lied.* 'He says bad things about God and claims that Jesus will tear down our Temple!' they fibbed.

'Is this true?' asked the High Priest.

Everyone looked at Stephen. He didn't look like a man facing a death sentence for a crime he hadn't committed. Instead, his face shone with an unearthly beauty – he looked like an angel! No one who saw him ever forgot that face. 'Listen,' said Stephen, and the whole courtroom leaned forward to listen as Stephen retold the story of their people: Abraham and God's promise, Joseph and his jealous brothers, Moses and the miraculous escape from Egypt, the Ten Commandments and the Temple in Jerusalem.** Stephen reminded his people

---

* A person can be accused of *blasphemy* if they insult God or holy things. In Jesus' time, blasphemy was a serious religious crime.
** You can read about Abraham in *The crucial cut*, Joseph in *Good news, bad news* and the Ten Commandments in *Laws for living*, all in **Beastly Bible Stories 2**. You can read about Moses in *The Great Escape* in **Beastly Bible Stories 4** and about the Temple in *Gold galore!* in **Beastly Bible Stories 3**.

of all the prophets they'd killed who had promised a Messiah.* 'And **YOU LOT** killed the **MESSIAH HIMSELF**!' he said.

'**BOOOOOOOO**!' hollered the crowd. Everyone in the courtroom was furious with Stephen, but Stephen himself was full of the Holy Spirit.

Then he gasped in wonder. '**LOOK**!' he said, pointing upwards. 'I can see heaven opening! I can see the **GLORY OF GOD** – and there's **JESUS**, standing right next to him!'

'**AAAAAAARGH**!' roared the crowd, trying to drown out Stephen's words. '**GETTIM**!' The whole courtroom became a mad mob that rushed towards Stephen and dragged him out of the city. '**BLASPHEMER**!' they yelled. '**STONE HIM**!'

The witnesses who had lied about Stephen tore off their coats and left them with a fierce-looking young man. They rolled up their sleeves, grabbed the sharpest stones they could find, took aim and – **THUNK**! The first stone knocked Stephen to his knees and he began to pray, 'Lord Jesus, don't hold this sin against them!' Then 20 more stones flew through the air, followed by 30 more, until Stephen was stone dead.

---

*You can read about them in *Powerful Prophets* in **Beastly Bible Stories 1**.

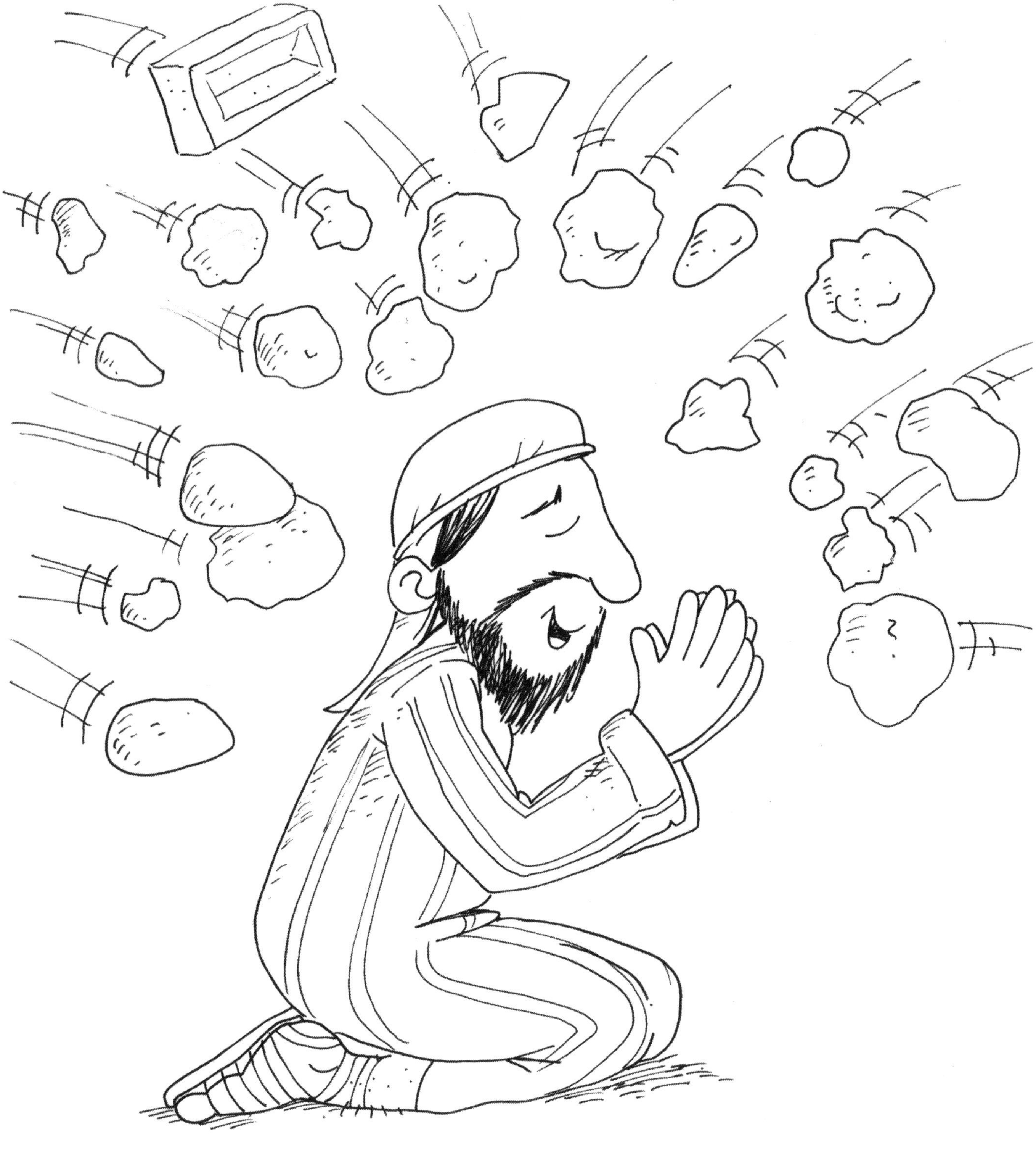

Killer Saul

The fierce-looking young man who had been left holding the coats watched and smiled grimly. *Serves him right!* he thought. *One less Christian for me to find!* He was Saul of Tarsus, a Roman citizen and super-strict Pharisee who passionately protected the Jewish Law. It was his job to hunt down and destroy anyone who dared to believe in Jesus. Christian kids probably called him 'Killer Saul' (because he wanted to kill us all – geddit?). But Saul's work was no joke: he tore the Church apart by raiding houses, interrogating families and dragging men and women off to prison.

The very day that Stephen died, Saul went through Jerusalem like a guided missile. He wouldn't stop until he had completely destroyed his target: Team Jesus.

This story shows that the Holy Spirit is unstoppable: the inspired disciples spoke out about Jesus, healed people in his name and grew the new Church in spite of their enemies. It seemed as if nothing could stand in their way, but one man was determined to try. Read on to find out what Killer Saul did next . . .

You can read about these daring disciples and the death of Stephen in Acts 3–7.

TOTAL TURNAROUND
Saul becomes a new man

Target Damascus

'I'LL KILL EVERY LAST CHRISTIAN!' Saul of Tarsus was a man on a mission: he would stop at nothing to crush the Church. Now he was on the way to Damascus, armed with search warrants for the synagogues and some big bullies who would drag any Jesus-loving Jews off to Jerusalem in chains. Saul strode towards Damascus like a wolf with his pack in search of prey.

Suddenly – **PIIZZAAAAAP!** A blindingly bright light flashed in Saul's face. He fell down, clutching his eyes. Then a one-of-a-kind Voice said, 'SAUL, SAUL, WHY ARE YOU ATTACKING ME?'

Saul whispered, 'Who are you, Lord?'

'I AM JESUS – the one you're attacking! Now get up and go to the city. You'll be told what to do next.'

Then there was silence. The big bullies who were travelling with Saul were stunned. They had heard the one-of-a-kind Voice but they hadn't seen a thing! What was going on? Whatever it was, it had brought their boss to his knees, so they went to help him up – but when he stared at them with wide, white, unseeing eyes, they realised he'd gone **BLIND!**

So Saul's men led him into the city like a blind beggar and found him a place to stay. For three days he saw nothing, ate nothing and drank nothing at all.

A changed man

Meanwhile, the Jesus-lovers in the city were hiding. They had heard rumours that Killer Saul was on his way and they weren't taking any chances. One disciple was asleep in his sister's cellar when a Voice which was louder than thunder and gentler than a lullaby called his name: '**ANANIAS!**'

'I'm here, Lord!'

'Get up now and go to Judas' house in Straight Street,' said Jesus. 'Ask for a man from Tarsus called Saul. He'll be praying, and he's waiting for you, because I told him in a vision that you would come and cure his blindness.'

Ananias gulped. 'Lord, surely you don't mean **THE** Saul of Tarsus? Killer Saul? But he's a monster! He's done terrible things to true Christian believers, and now he's here to drag more of us off to Jerusalem!'

But Jesus said, '**GO!** I have picked Saul to work for me. He will tell everyone about me: non-Jews, kings and the whole of Israel! And he'll suffer for my sake.'

Shaking, Ananias went to Straight Street and knocked on the door. *What if this is some kind of trap?* he wondered. But when he saw the trembling man kneeling in the corner, his heart melted. Saul turned at the sound of footsteps and stared with wide, white, unseeing eyes. Ananias touched him gently and said, 'Brother Saul, the Lord Jesus has appeared to you – now he has sent me, so that you may **SEE AGAIN** and be **FILLED** with the **HOLY SPIRIT**!'

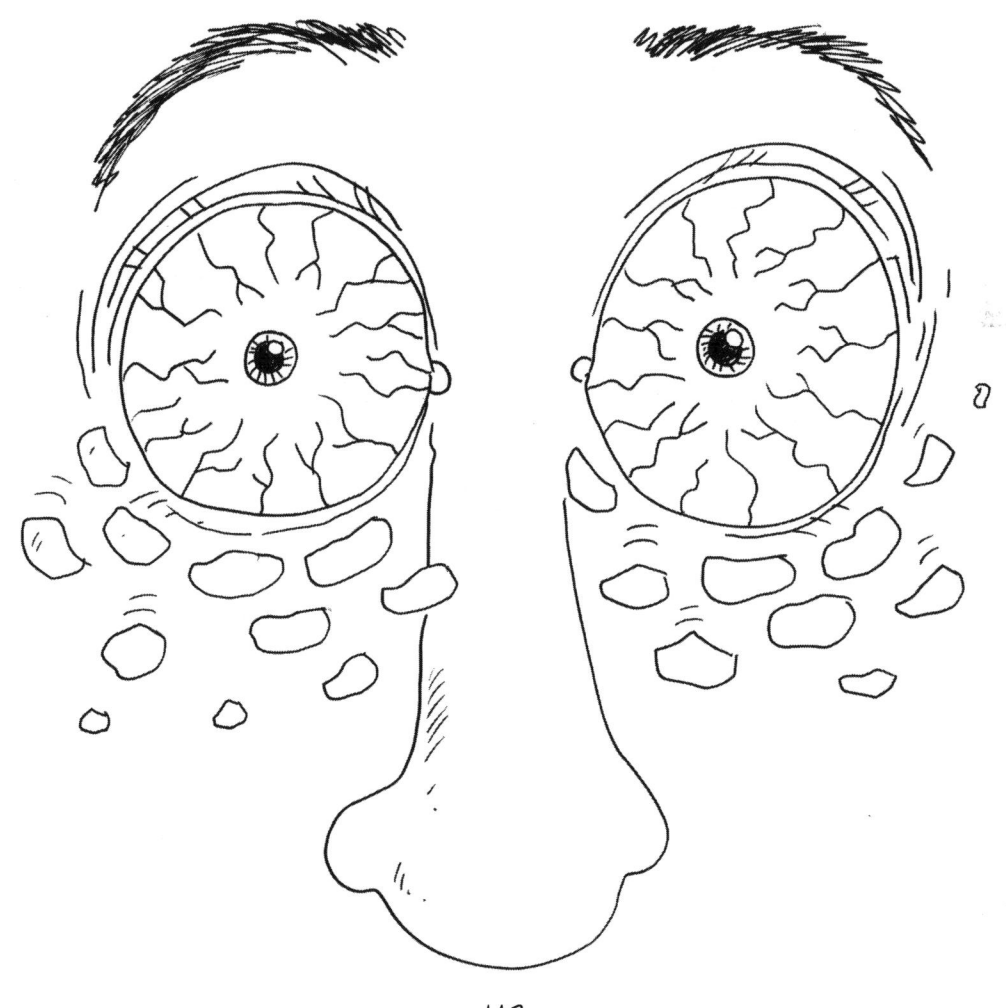

PLIIISP! Straight away, silvery-white flakes like fish scales peeled off Saul's eyes and he could see again! The very first thing he did was to get baptised. **SPLOOOSH!** Then he ate and drank for the first time in three days, and started to get his strength back. Killer Saul was a new man: he had changed from being a hard-line Jesus-hater to a full-on Jesus-lover. Later he would take a new name: Paul.

The new recruit

As soon as Saul was strong enough, he did what he had come to Damascus to do, which was to visit all the synagogues and talk about Jesus. But instead of questioning the Jews and jailing suspected Jesus-lovers, he stood up and declared, 'JESUS IS THE SON OF GOD!'

The Jews were amazed and confused. 'Isn't this the man who tore the Church apart in Jerusalem?' they asked each other. 'Didn't he come here deliberately to destroy anyone who's a member of Team Jesus? Is this some kind of trap?'

But Saul said, 'JESUS IS THE MESSIAH!'

Within days, the Jews in Damascus were plotting to kill Saul. They surrounded the place where he was staying, but Jesus' followers smuggled him over the wall in a laundry basket and sneaked him away.

In Jerusalem, Saul went straight to the disciples and said, 'I'm one of you!' But the disciples were not so sure. *Really?* they thought. *Killer Saul, a member of Team Jesus? It's got to be a trap!* But Barnabas, the disciple, spoke up for Saul and told everyone what had happened to him in Damascus. So Saul joined the disciples, and before long he was standing in Jerusalem shouting, 'JESUS IS THE SON OF GOD! JESUS IS THE MESSIAH!' Saul argued fiercely about God with everyone, and before long the Jews *and* the Greeks wanted to kill him! The disciples smuggled their troublemaking new recruit back home to Tarsus for the time being.

Meanwhile, the new Church was busy loving God and, being filled with the Holy Spirit, it grew and grew.

So Jesus' greatest enemy became his biggest fan! After this amazing conversion, Saul/Paul became the hero of the early Church. No one travelled further or spread the good news about Jesus more eagerly than he did. The letters he wrote to guide the first Christians are so important that they are part of the Bible's New Testament today. Read on for more adventures!

You can read about Saul's conversion to Christianity in Acts 9:1-31.

TUCK IN!
No more food rules

Peter's picnic

GR-GR-GROOOOAAARGH! Peter's tummy rumbled loudly, but he ignored it and went on praying. Even up here on the roof he could smell the bread that was baking for dinner. His mouth watered, so he looked up and concentrated hard on God. Suddenly – **WOOOOOMPF!** – a giant tablecloth appeared in the sky! It was coming closer, its corners held up by invisible hands. Peter could see that it was full of something: the cloth was bulging with big lumps that wriggled and heaved. It came closer and closer until it touched the ground and spread itself out in front of Peter like a picnic rug.

'**EEUUCH!**' Peter jumped backwards – there was no way he'd eat *this* picnic! There were live lizards! Bats, bugs and badgers! Snakes and seagulls! Camels and crocodiles! There were even *pigs*! These creatures were climbing all over each other, and the picnic rug was covered in paw prints and trotter tracks. For a faithful Jew who had always followed the food rules,* this picnic was a nightmare! Peter shuddered.

---

* In Jewish Law, eating certain animals is forbidden, including pigs, anything with paws, anything creepy or crawly, birds of prey and creatures like camels with the wrong kind of hooves. You can read about the food rules in *Clean and unclean* in **Beastly Bible Stories 2**.

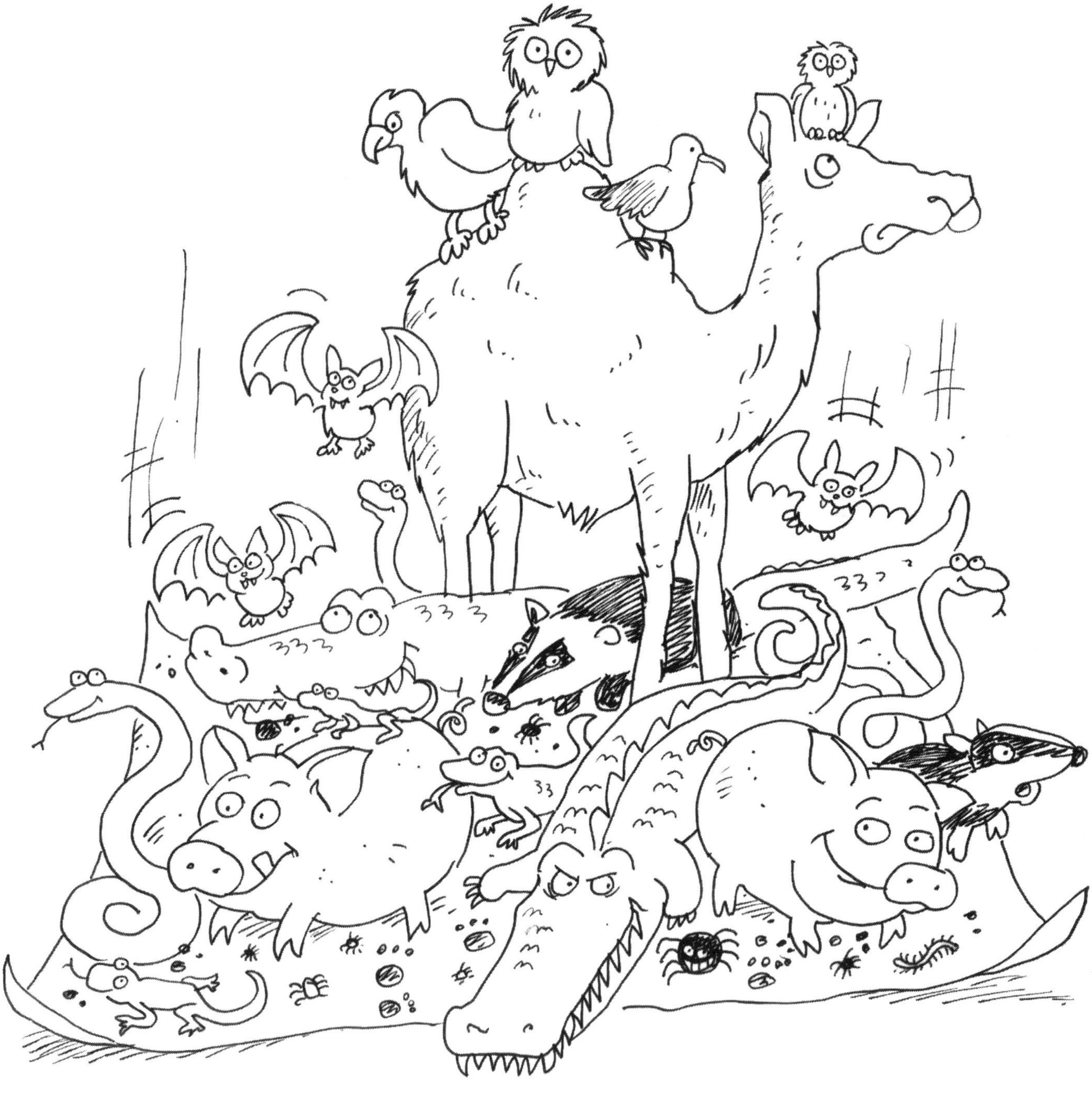

Then a one-of-a-kind Voice said, 'Tuck in, Peter! Kill something and eat it!'

Peter replied, '**NO WAY, LORD**! I've never eaten anything unclean!'

Then the Voice that was gentler than a lullaby but louder than thunder said, '**IF GOD HAS MADE SOMETHING CLEAN, YOU MUST NOT CALL IT UNCLEAN!**'

Peter argued once, twice, three times, but God insisted: '**YOU MUST NOT CALL IT UNCLEAN!**' And **WOOOOOMPF!** – the giant tablecloth with its disgusting dinner disappeared into the sky.

KNOCK KNOCK KNOCK! There was someone at the gate, but Peter's head was still full of the vision he'd seen. *What does it mean?* he wondered. Then the Holy Spirit gave Peter his orders: 'There are three men at the gate! Get up now and go with them, because I've sent them to you!'

Sure enough, the three men were asking for Peter. They said, 'Cornelius, our master, the Roman centurion, is good and kind. He believes in God and wants you to come to his house!' This may not sound like a big deal to you, but it was against Jewish law to hang out with non-Jews (or *Gentiles*) because they were unclean. However, Peter still had God's words ringing in his ears ('**IF GOD HAS MADE SOMETHING CLEAN, YOU MUST NOT CALL IT UNCLEAN!**'), so he did as the Holy Spirit said and headed to the centurion's house, taking six of his Jesus-loving Jewish friends with him.

Romans welcome

Cornelius the centurion was thrilled to welcome Peter and his friends. 'I was saying my prayers,' he said, 'when suddenly this person in shining white clothes appeared in front of me! He told me to send for you and listen to what God wants you to say! And here you are!' The centurion's friends and family all looked expectantly at Peter.

'Um,' said Peter. He looked around him at all the smiling Gentiles and the first non-Jewish house he'd ever been in. 'Er,' he said, and swallowed. Then the Holy Spirit, who had taught him to speak at Pentecost, gave him the words he needed. 'Now I get it!' he said. **GOD DOESN'T HAVE FAVOURITES**! Whoever you are, if you love God and do good, then that's fine by God!'

Huh?!? thought his Jesus-loving Jewish friends. *But Jesus is OUR Messiah! Aren't WE his favourites?*

Peter went on, 'You all **KNOW** that Jesus is Lord! John baptised him and God gave him the Holy Spirit,* and he went about healing and teaching! We saw it all – and we saw them kill him on a cross in Jerusalem! God brought him back from the dead, and he ate and drank with us! We are his witnesses – he told us to tell everyone about him! He is the Chosen One who will judge the living and the dead! He forgives the sins of everyone who believes in him!'

* You can read about this in *The Saviour gets a soaking* in **Beastly Bible Stories 5**.

WHOOOOOSH! The Gentiles listened to Peter with open mouths, and suddenly they felt wonderfully strong as the Holy Spirit breathed into them. '**PRAISE THE LORD!**' they shouted. '**JESUS IS LORD! PRAISE BE TO GOD!**' – although what actually came out of their mouths was something like, '**KOH-dah-rah SHOH-kr!**' or '**MAHG-duh lah rahp!**' or '**Ki-reon Yess-oun!**' or '**Louse DAY-oh!**'

Peter's Jesus-loving Jewish friends heard the Gentiles speaking different languages, just as the disciples had done at Pentecost, and were completely dumbstruck: *What?!?* they thought. *Isn't the Holy Spirit just for Jews? Isn't that God's gift to US?*

But Peter shouted, 'Come on, let's get these guys wet! If they've got the Holy Spirit, just like us, then how can we *not* baptise them?!' **SPLOOOSH! SPLOOOSH! SPLOOOSH!** So Peter and the disciples baptised all the new Christians in the centurion's house.

Everyone welcome!

The story travelled to Jerusalem, quick as a newsflash: **GENTILES ACCEPT JESUS AS LORD! NON-JEWS CAN JOIN THE CHURCH!** The Jesus-loving Jews argued with Peter, saying, 'How could you go to a Roman's house?! How could you eat his unclean food?!'

But Peter told them about his vision of the heavenly picnic and the one-of-a-kind Voice that had said, '**IF GOD HAS MADE SOMETHING CLEAN, YOU MUST NOT CALL IT UNCLEAN!**' Peter said, 'So if God says that Gentiles and their food are clean, how can we say they're unclean? And if he's given his Holy Spirit to Jesus-loving non-Jews, then **HOW CAN WE STAND IN GOD'S WAY?!**'

There was silence: ' ' In the silence, the Holy Spirit worked whisperingly to make everyone understand. Then, '**PRAISE THE LORD!**' shouted the Jesus-loving Jews. 'That means **EVERYONE** can be forgiven and find new life! **HOORAY!**'

This was a very important moment for the Church and for Christianity. The Jews were God's Chosen People and Jesus was one of them, but he had always helped and healed people who were outsiders.* In this story, God gave his Holy Spirit to the Gentiles, and Peter opened the Church to non-Jews and anyone who believes in Jesus – including us, today. It also explains why Christians don't follow Jewish food rules any more!

You can read this story in Acts 10–11.

---

* You can read about this in *Outrageous outsiders* in **Beastly Bible Stories 6**.

TURNING THE WORLD UPSIDE DOWN

ANGELIC ESCAPE
Peter busts out of prison

Herod on the warpath

Did you know there is more than one King Herod in the Bible? The Herods were mostly horrible. There was King Herod who killed all the baby boys in Bethlehem; his son, King Herod who beheaded John the Baptiser;* and his nephew, King Herod who stars in this story. This King Herod kicked off by attacking the new Christians and killing James, the brother of John, with a sword. **SPLUNCH!**

Many of the Jews celebrated when they heard what had happened to one of Jesus' closest friends – half of the pair he'd nicknamed 'the Thunder Boys'. '**HOORAY!**' they cheered. '**LONG LIVE KING HEROD!**' Herod enjoyed the applause so much that he wondered what he could do for an encore – so he arrested Peter and put him in prison. It was nearly the Passover Festival, which Herod reckoned would be the perfect time to show Peter off to the crowds – they'd love him for it! So Herod sent soldiers and the Church sent

---

* You can read about these Herods in *The baby-killing king* and *Killer Queen* in **Beastly Bible Stories 5**.

prayers. Day and night, four security squads guarded Peter, and the Christians asked God to help him.

Heaven-sent

'NGAAARGH... NGAAARGH... NGAAARGH...'

The soldiers' snores bounced off the walls of the high-security prison cell. That night, not one but two guards slept beside Peter, and the prisoner himself dozed awkwardly with both his arms chained to the wall. If you'd been there, you wouldn't have seen anything in the dark, but you'd have heard his uncomfortable snores: 'HNNNNARGH... kerCLANK... HNNNNARGH... kerCLINK...'

Suddenly there was someone else in the prison cell – an **ANGEL**! Instead of appearing with a **PHOOOM**! in a solid wall of light (which he could have done, easily) this angel came quietly and glowed gently, so as not to wake the guards. He tapped Peter on the shoulder and whispered, 'Get up! Quick!' Peter's eyes snapped open and he gasped. The angel put a finger on the prisoner's lips, and at his touch, the heavy iron chains became as limp as ribbons and simply fell off Peter's wrists: **kerCLUNK!**

The angel said, 'Come on, get dressed! Sandals on, now!' Peter did as he was told. 'Now wrap your cloak around you and come with me!' said the angel.

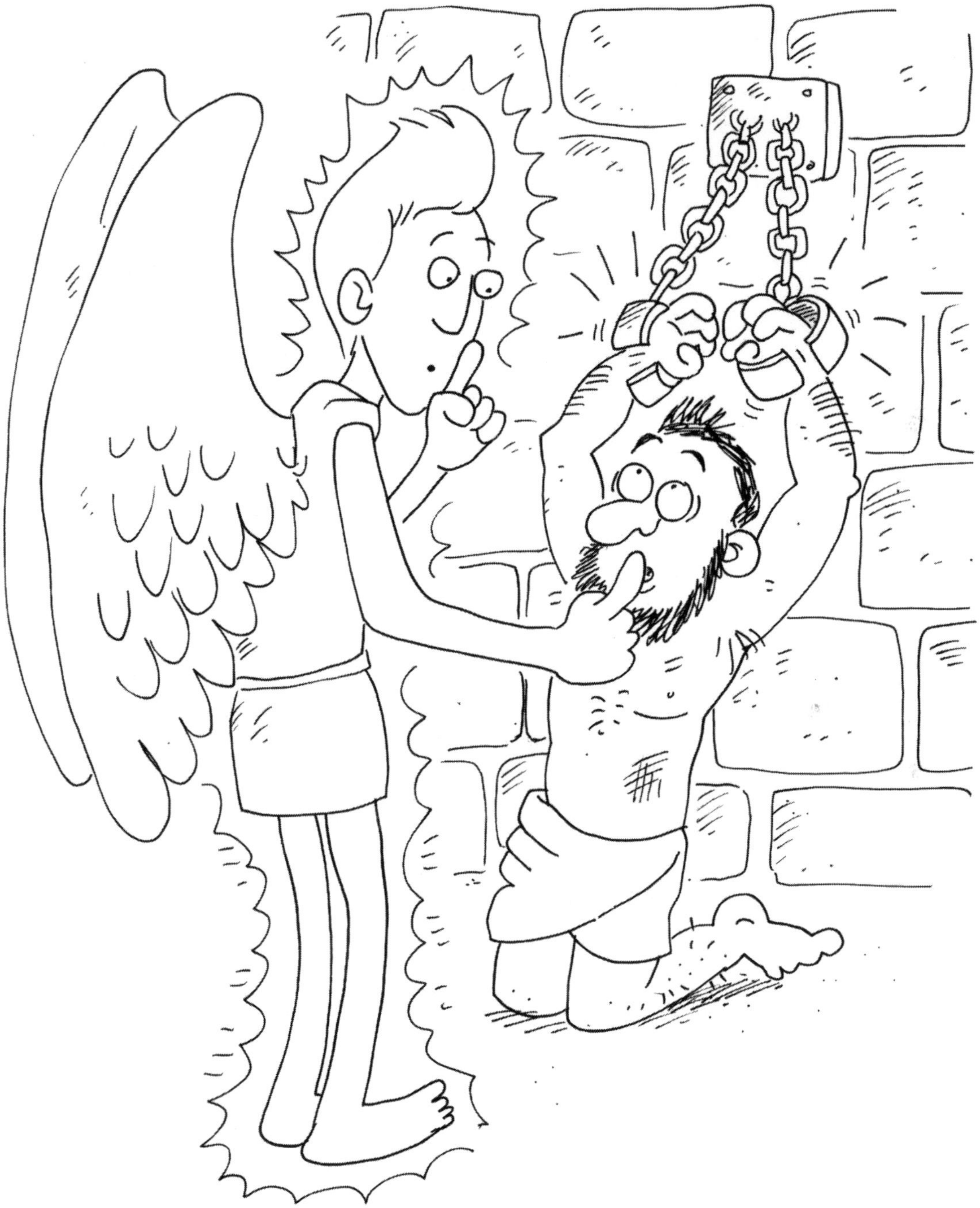

Like a sleepwalker, Peter followed the angel past the two snoring guards in his cell and past the squad of soldiers outside the door. *This can't be real!* thought Peter. *I must be dreaming!* The next thing he knew, he and the angel were approaching the main gate of the prison, which was bolted shut with big iron bars: as they got closer, the gate simply swung open by itself. They walked outside into the city and down a back street. Suddenly, as quietly as he had come, the angel disappeared.

Peter looked at the empty street outside the prison. He listened to the silence that was a world away from the guards' snores. He felt the raw rings on his wrists where the iron chains had been. '**WOAH!**' he said out loud. '**IT'S TRUE! GOD** really did send an **ANGEL** to rescue me!'

Safe house

Peter rushed straight to the house where he knew lots of his friends would be praying together. It was the middle of the night, but he hammered on the gate: **BAM! BAM-BAM-BAM BAM!** A little servant girl called Rhoda came running. '**WHO IS IT?**' she yelled. 'Don't you know what time it is?'

'**LET ME IN!**' shouted Peter. 'Something amazing's happened!'

Rhoda recognised Peter's voice and immediately ran back to his friends, shouting, '**PETER'S BACK!**'

But they said, '**YOU'RE BONKERS!**'

'I'm **NOT!**' she said. 'He's at the gate now!'

'It can't be him!' they said. 'You're **HEARING** things!'

Meanwhile, Peter was still knocking: **BAM! BAM-BAM-BAM BAM!** Everyone rushed to open the gate, and when they saw Peter standing there, they all started asking questions at once: 'But **HOW?** But **WHEN?** But **WHO?**'

'**SSSHHHH!**' said Peter, and told them the amazing story of the angel who'd rescued him from prison.

The next morning, just imagine the panic at the prison! Guards asleep on duty! Broken chains! And worst of all, a prize prisoner **GONE!** Herod was **FURIOUS!** He sent out search parties – **NOTHING!** He interrogated the guards – **NOTHING!** So he gave the order – '**KILL THEM ALL!**' – and four squads of soldiers were executed. '**THAT'LL TEACH THEM!**' snarled Herod.

Meanwhile, Peter the escaped prisoner quietly left town.

Beastly bonus – the end of Herod

Herod was now in a thoroughly bad mood. He sat on his throne in all his royal robes and sulked. When foreign ambassadors came to ask for his help, he let them grovel, flatter and beg. In the end he cleared his throat and began to speak. '**KING HEROD HEARS YOUR PATHETIC PLEADING!**' he said.

The people were so eager to please him that they interrupted, crying out, 'LISTEN! THE GREAT KING IS MORE THAN HUMAN – HE SPEAKS WITH THE VOICE OF A GOD!'

Herod smiled smugly and didn't contradict them. Suddenly – **PHOOOM!** The angel was back, this time in a solid wall of light. Now he was neither quiet nor gentle. **SMAACK!** The angel whacked Herod because he had tried to claim God's glory as his own. Immediately, a wiggling mass of worms devoured the king! All that was left of the mighty Herod was a pile of bones and an empty throne.*

Meanwhile, the good news about Jesus continued to spread and, being filled with new followers, the Church grew and grew.

This story is a reminder that the new Church faced some powerful enemies, and from the beginning Christians risked imprisonment and death. However, Peter's adventures show that once again nothing can stand in the way of God and his plans for the Church, which carried on growing and gathering new believers.

You can read this story in Acts 12.

---

* Do you remember what Jesus' mum said the Messiah would do? 'He'll put powerful people in their place!' That's just what has happened here… You can read more about this in *Awesome angels* in **Beastly Bible Stories 5**.

PRISON BREAK QUAKE
Paul and Silas behind bars

Fortune-telling fan

'Listen to these men and be **SAVED**!' the slave girl screamed. 'Listen to these men and be **SAVED**!' She pointed at Saul (who now used his Roman name, Paul) and his friend Silas, who had just arrived in the Roman city of Philippi to be greeted by their biggest and loudest fan. 'They are the **GREAT GOD'S SERVANTS**!' she yelled. 'Listen to these men and be **SAVED**!'

Paul and Silas looked at each other. They had already seen so many cities, baptised so many new believers and escaped such angry protests by non-believers that they thought they knew what to expect. They always began by telling people the good news about Jesus, but now Silas grumbled, 'No one will be able to listen to us at all if she keeps up that racket!'

It wasn't the slave girl's fault. A soothsaying spirit was controlling her, and her owners made pots of money from her fortune-telling talents. The spirit inside her saw God at work in Paul and Silas, and it made her follow them everywhere, yelling, 'They are the **GREAT GOD'S SERVANTS**!

Listen to these men and be SAVED! Listen to these men and BE SAVED! LISTEN TO THESE MEN AND BE SAVED!' Just imagine hearing that all day, every day, from the minute you woke up – 'LISTEN TO THESE MEN AND BE SAVED!' – to the moment you fell asleep – 'LISTEN TO THESE MEN AND BE SAVED!'

It drove Paul nuts, and finally he snapped. He said to the soothsaying spirit, 'In the name of JESUS CHRIST, I order you to GET OUT!' and WOOOMPF! the spirit vanished, leaving behind a very tired slave girl who didn't know where her next meal was coming from, let alone what your fortune might be. Her queues of customers disappeared and her money-grabbing owners were FURIOUS!

'GET THEM!' they yelled, and dragged Paul and Silas to the town hall to see the local judges. 'THESE MEN HAVE BEEN TURNING THE WORLD UPSIDE DOWN, AND NOW THEY'RE TRYING TO DO THE SAME TO OUR CITY!' shouted the slave owners.

'BOOOOO!' jeered the crowd.

'THEY'RE ANTI-ROMAN!' screamed the slave owners.

'BOOOOO! RAAAAARGH!' roared the crowd.

Faced with this angry mob, the judges made a decision. They stripped the tunics from the prisoners' backs – **RIIIISP!** – and declared, '**BEAT THEM!**' **WHAP! WHAP! WHAP! WHAP! WHAP! WHAP!** Paul and Silas were whipped and then sent to prison. The judges said to the warden, 'Keep a careful eye on this pair – they're trouble!' So the warden ordered his guards to lock the prisoners in a high-security cell and fasten their feet in wooden stocks. **KerCLANK! KerCLINK!** Paul and Silas weren't going anywhere.

Behind bars

'Praise the **LOOORD! AAAAAAAALLELUUUUUIA!**' It was midnight in the prison and Silas was singing, but none of the other prisoners minded, because he had a beautiful voice. They closed their eyes and listened. 'The **LORD** is my **SHEEEPHERD!**' sang Silas, while Paul prayed: '**SAVE US**, O Lord! Hurry up and **HELP US! RUIN** your enemies and make those who love you **REJOICE!**'

'**AMEN!**' chorused all the prisoners.

Suddenly – **BRRROOOOOAAAGHGHGH!!** Watch out! **EARTHQUAKE!** The massive tremor shook the prison to its foundations, and the walls wobbled like a tent on a windy day.

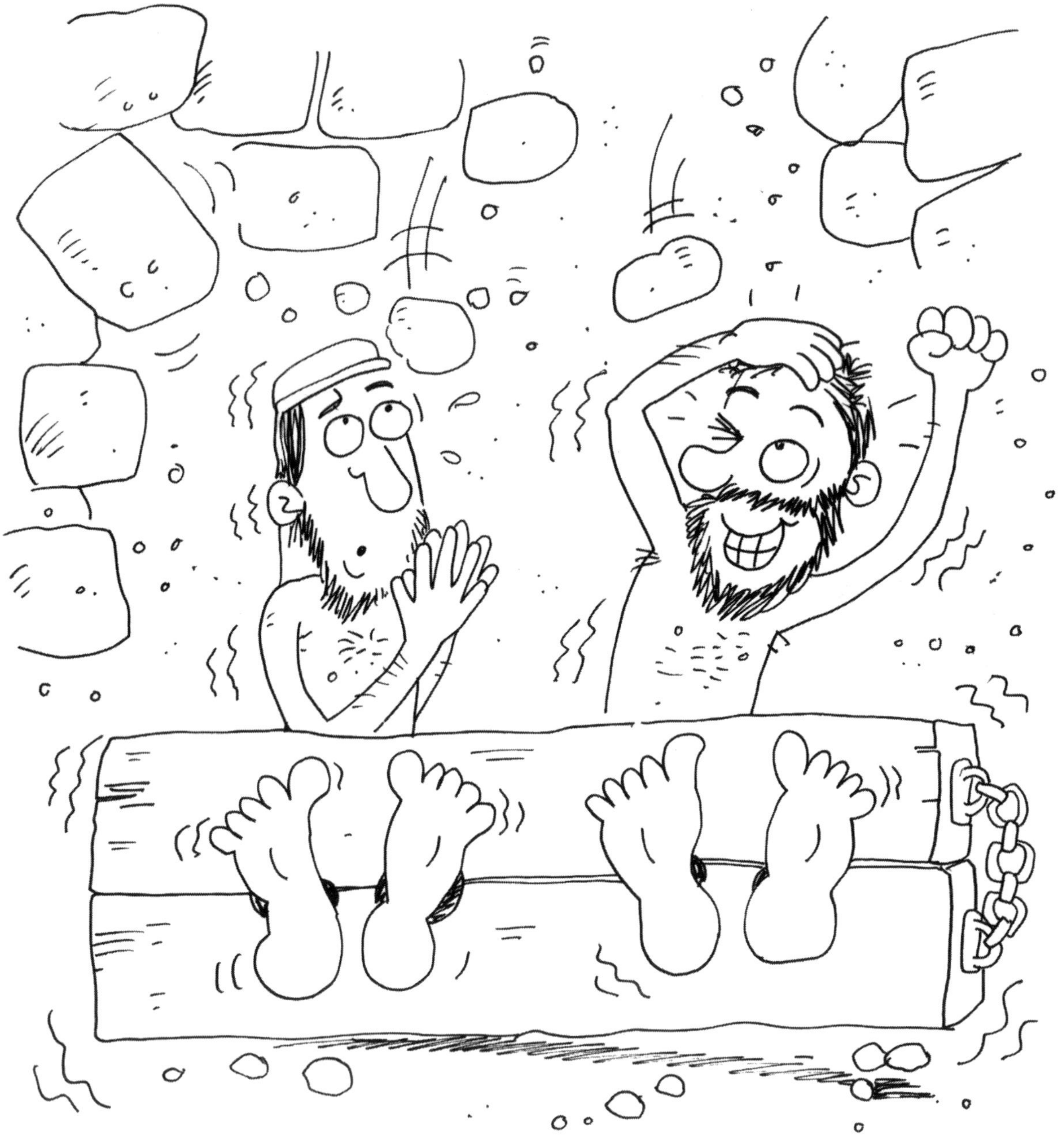

Ker-CLANG! All the prison gates burst open. **KerCLUNK! KerCLUNK! KerCLUNK!** Everyone's chains fell off. '**HOOORAY!**' cheered the prisoners, and hugged each other.

At that moment the prison warden woke up. He saw the gates of the prison standing wide open and thought that all the prisoners had escaped. 'On my watch, too!' he wailed. 'I'm a failure!'

Being a good Roman, he drew his sword and was ready to fall on the pointy end on purpose – put Paul rushed towards him, shouting, '**DON'T DO IT!** You're not a failure – **LOOK!** We're all still here!'

The warden looked up to see all his prisoners smiling at him, and he realised that God was at work. He fell at Paul and Silas' feet saying, 'My lords, how can I be saved? Tell me what to do!'

Paul replied, '**BELIEVE IN THE LORD JESUS, AND YOU WILL BE SAVED** – you and your whole family!'

A new church is born

So Paul and Silas became honoured guests in the prison warden's house, and they told all his family and servants the good news about Jesus. The warden himself washed the wounds left by the whip, and Paul and Silas baptised everyone in the house. **SPLOOOSH! SPLOOOSH!**

SPLOOOSH! Then everyone stayed up all night and celebrated with a fantastic family feast!

In the morning, a message came for the prison warden from the judges: 'Paul and Silas have been punished enough. Release them and tell them to go quietly.'

But Paul said, '**NO WAY!** They've got to come and say **SORRY** to **US!** We are **ROMAN CITIZENS** and they beat us and imprisoned us without trial! We're not going quietly – we want a **PUBLIC APOLOGY!**'

When the judges heard what they'd done to a pair of Roman citizens, they panicked. 'Please!' they said to Paul and Silas, 'Forgive us! We're really sorry!' The judges' reputations were ruined. Meanwhile, Paul and Silas cheered up the new church in Philippi before they left, and all the new believers rejoiced: '**HALLELUJAH! PRAISE THE LORD!**'

So Paul's prayer in prison was answered, and the church in Philippi was the first church established by Paul in Europe. He loved it very much and kept in touch – the Bible even contains the letter he wrote to encourage the Christians there after he'd left! You can read this in Philippians.

You can read this story in Acts 16.

FROM STRENGTH TO STRENGTH
The good news keeps on spreading

Extraordinary Ephesus

WHHHOOOSH! The Holy Spirit was blowing like a whirlwind across the world, driving forward the disciples, blowing away people's old beliefs and carrying the seeds of the Christian Church wherever it went. The Holy Spirit pushed Paul to Asia,* where he preached about Jesus and persuaded loads of locals – Jews and Greeks – to become Christians. **SPLOOOSH! SPLOOOSH! SPLOOOSH!** For two years he was busy baptising, and like a well-watered seed the Church grew and grew.

In a place called Ephesus, God made some mind-blowing miracles happen through Paul – and even through his dirty washing! A man with a revolting rash touched Paul's face flannel, and **SWOOOSH!** His skin was suddenly soft and smooth again. A woman with an evil spirit touched Paul's manky hanky, and **WOOMPF!** The spirit disappeared like a bad smell.

* The Bible's name for modern-day Turkey.

When the local magicians saw these amazing miracles, they tried to steal some of Paul's power for themselves. Seven sorcerers went to work on one man who had been invaded by an evil spirit. '**BE GONE!**' they said to the spirit. 'We order you in the name of **JESUS**, whom **PAUL** preaches about!'

But the spirit answered, 'I know Jesus and I know Paul, but **WHO DO YOU THINK YOU ARE?**' Then the man who was driven by the evil spirit suddenly leapt on the sorcerers: '**RAAAAAAAARGH!**'

It was seven against one but the spirit was stronger. **BIFF! WHAP! OOOFF! THWAPP! BAM! UGGH!** Before long, the bare and bleeding sorcerers burst out of the house and ran for their lives: '**AAAAAIIIEEEEEE!**'

When word got out, all the local Jesus-lovers praised the Lord, and all the magicians completely lost faith in their own magic. They knew real power when they saw it, so they built a bonfire and burned all their books of spells. Sorcery worth 50,000 silver coins went up in smoke! The word of the Lord had won, and the Church grew stronger every day.

The deadly sermon

The Holy Spirit never stays still: the good news keeps on going, and so did Paul. He sent his helpers on ahead, then he pressed on to Macedonia, then to Greece and back again, bucking up new believers (and also making enemies) wherever he went. He narrowly escaped a plot to kill him before he turned up in Troas, where he met many other disciples.

The night before Paul left Troas, everyone got together for dinner. Servants carried the food up three flights of stairs to Paul and his friends, but Paul wasn't ready to eat yet. There was so much to say to his fellow Jesus-lovers before he left! Paul started to preach. As it began to get dark, the servants carried more lamps up the three flights of stairs and wondered whether the guests would ever eat the food that was waiting on the tables; Paul carried on talking. The room got hotter with so many lamps, and people opened the shutters to let in the cool night air; Paul carried on talking.

One young man called Eutychus was so hot and tired that he sat in the open window and leant against the wall while Paul (you guessed it) carried on talking. Eutychus let his eyes droop, then he began to doze – then he nodded off and fell backwards out of the window, three floors up! '**AAAAIIIIIEEEEEE!**' he screamed as he woke up. **THWUMP!** He hit the ground head first. His friends raced downstairs, but when they found him lying there as twisted as a broken doll, they knew he was dead. They looked at each other in horror as they carefully lifted Eutychus' body from the ground.

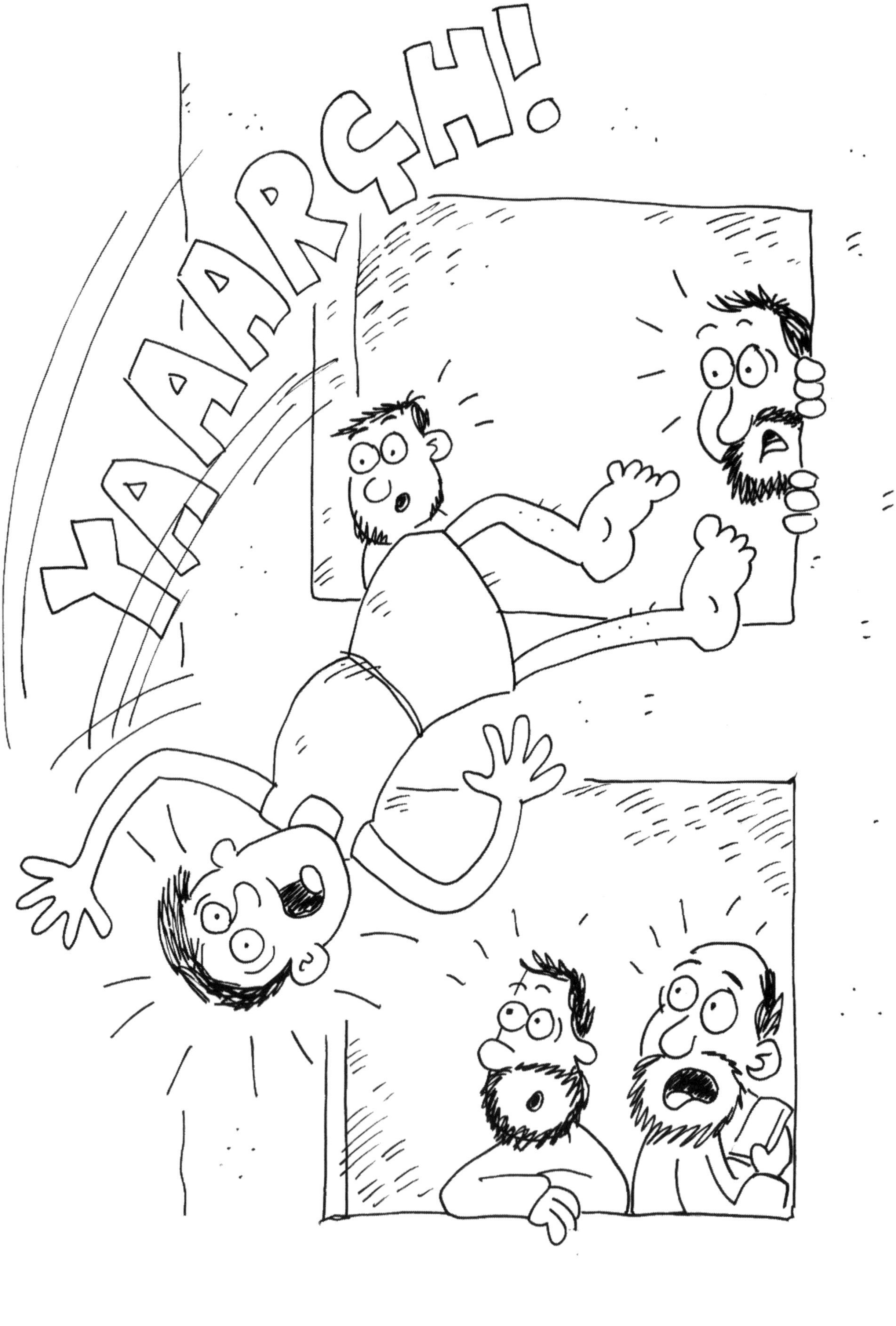
YAAARGH!

Paul was right behind them. He went straight to the dead man, gathered him up in his arms and said to the onlookers, 'Don't be scared – he's alive!' And so he was – just like that! Eutychus' delighted friends hurried home with him, and he walked and talked all the way.

Paul went back upstairs, where at long last he decided it was time for dinner. He broke the bread and blessed it, then the disciples all ate together. Everyone perked up and Paul carried on talking. He talked all night, and finally said farewell to his friends in Troas as the sun came up. There were a lot more goodbyes to come . . .

When Paul saw his friends from Ephesus one last time, he said, 'The Holy Spirit is driving me forward to Jerusalem! I know that there's trouble ahead, but I don't care about myself – I just want to tell the world about Jesus and finish the race God has made me run!' He pointed at the leaders of the new church in Ephesus. 'Be good shepherds!' he said. 'Look after your sheep! Protect them from wolves and look after the weaklings! Now – goodbye! You will never see me again – but I'll write!' There were prayers, kisses and goodbye hugs all round as Paul continued on his long journey to Jerusalem.

Trouble ahead

Paul encountered so many dangers and difficulties on his journeys that his race to tell people about Jesus was more like an obstacle course. In one of his letters he made a list of everything he put up with:*

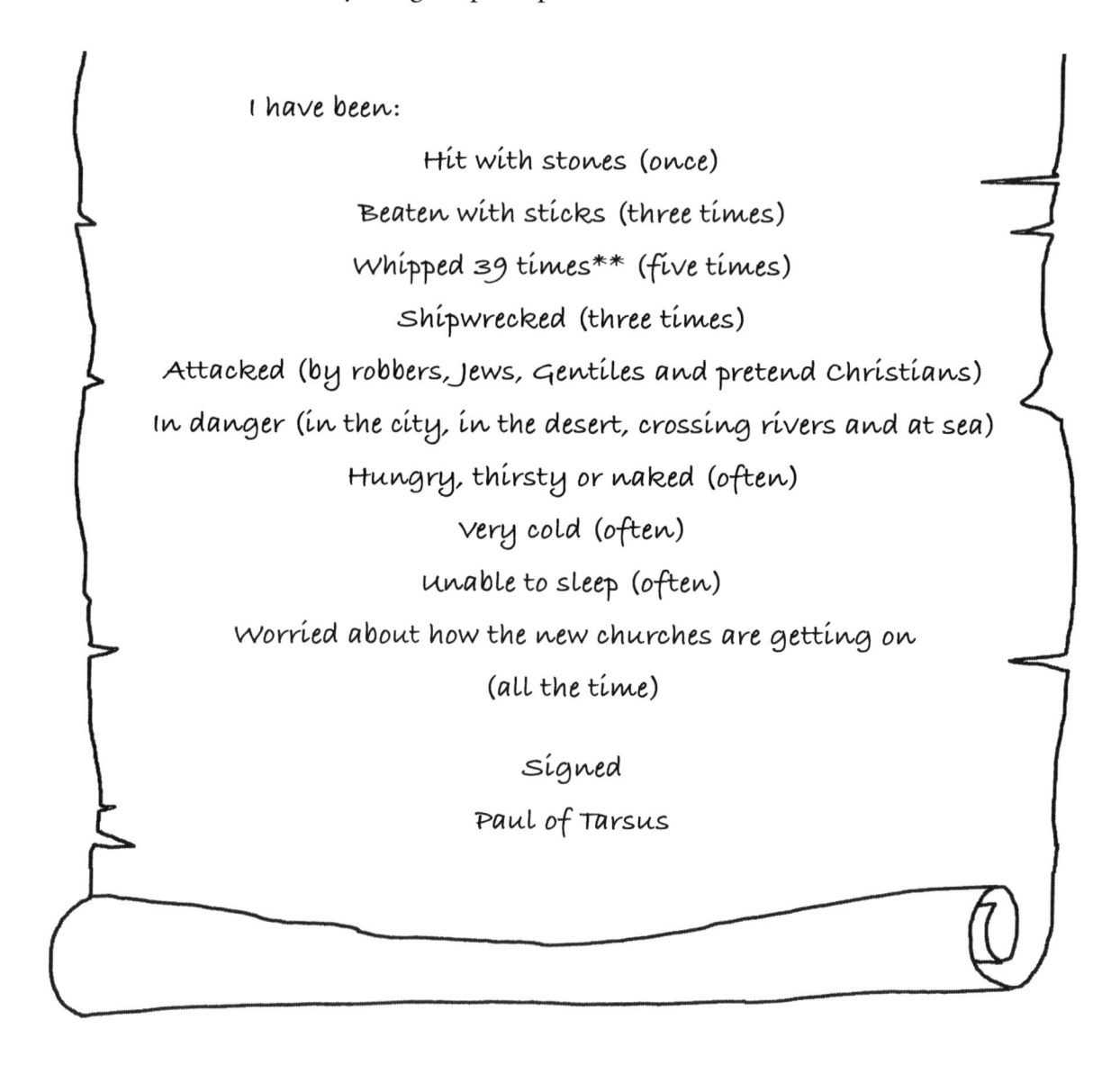

> I have been:
>
> Hit with stones (once)
> Beaten with sticks (three times)
> Whipped 39 times** (five times)
> Shipwrecked (three times)
> Attacked (by robbers, Jews, Gentiles and pretend Christians)
> In danger (in the city, in the desert, crossing rivers and at sea)
> Hungry, thirsty or naked (often)
> Very cold (often)
> Unable to sleep (often)
> Worried about how the new churches are getting on (all the time)
>
> Signed
> Paul of Tarsus

* 2 Corinthians 11.
** People believed that 40 lashes would kill a man, so 39 lashes was the next-worst punishment they could give.

In spite of all this, Paul never stopped serving God, loving Jesus and growing the new Church.

Paul finally reached Jerusalem, where he caused trouble in the Temple by turning up with non-Jewish Jesus-lovers to worship God. Roman soldiers arrested him before he could cause a riot, but as he was a Roman citizen, he demanded to be taken to Rome. So Paul's travels and preaching continued, although now he was a prisoner – an 'ambassador in chains' whose message was the good news about Jesus. He never did see Ephesus again, although his letter to the new Christians there is in the Bible: you can read it in Ephesians.

You can read about these adventures in Acts 19–20.

Shipwreck and Snakebite
Paul's adventures

Worse things happen at sea

'**ALL ABOARD!**' yelled the captain. 'No time to lose!' Prisoner Paul climbed up the gangplank with 276 other prisoners, guards and crew. The ship, with its belly full of grain, was bound for Rome – but that was far away on the other side of the sea, and it was late in the year for such a long trip. They would need to race to Rome or the autumn gales would get them first. Already the white-capped waves were squabbling under a stormy sky.

Paul stood on the deck with the wind behind him and spoke to the crew and the kind centurion in charge. 'Now listen to me,' he said. 'I see trouble ahead. We're in danger of losing everything on this trip: the cargo, the ship and even our lives!' But the captain and the navigator disagreed, so the centurion gave the order to depart immediately.

'**ANCHORS AWEIGH!**' shouted the crew, and the ship set sail. A steady south-westerly wind helped them along at first, but one morning the wind suddenly changed: **PHFOOOOOSH!** A hurricane pounced on the ship and hunted it like a tiger, snapping at its sails and ripping its timbers. **WHOO-OOOOSH!** The whirling wind surrounded the ship and threatened to run it aground. **SWOO-SPLOOOSH!** The waves battered the deck, while the crew threw the cargo overboard, followed by the ship's tackle. **BROOAAMMUMMM! BRRRROOAAAMMM!** Thunder rolled across the sea; storm clouds blotted out the sun and stars for three whole days. The passengers stopped eating and clung to each other: no one was coming to help them, and there was nothing to do but hang on and hope for the best.

Land ahoy!

Paul stood up and said, 'You should have listened to me! If we'd never left our last port, we wouldn't be in this mess now! But **BE BRAVE** – no one's going to die; we'll only lose this ship. You see, last night God sent me an angel who said, "Don't be afraid, Paul – whatever happens, you **WILL** get to Rome, and God will keep you and all your sailing companions safe." So you see? **ALL WILL BE WELL!** I trust God, and you'll see – we'll find some island sooner or later.'

A fortnight later the ship was still adrift, but in the middle of the night a sailor shouted, '**LAND AHOY!**'

The other sailors peered out into the dark. There was land, all right, but there were also some dirty great rocks. The sailors agreed, 'Let's ditch the ship and save ourselves!' They lowered the ship's dinghy down, ready to make their escape.

But Paul knew what was going on and he told the centurion, 'Keep them on board! If we lose the crew, none of us will survive!' So the centurion sent soldiers to cut the ropes and let the dinghy drift away without the deserters.

Before dawn, Paul woke everyone up. 'Come and have breakfast!' he said. 'It's time to get your strength up, because we're all going to leave this ship alive!' So he took bread, gave thanks and broke it, saying, 'Take some – come on, eat up!' Everyone did as Paul said – all 276 prisoners, guards and crew – and they felt much better for it.

As the sun came up, they could all see dry land, but the captain spotted something else. '**REEF AHEAD**!' he shouted. The crew did everything they could to steer them to safety, but **SSKKRRRUNCH**! With a terrible tearing noise, the ship ran aground and stuck fast. Waves battered the stern and the ship's timbers began to split.

'**ABANDON SHIP**!' shouted the crew.

The soldiers were ready to kill their prisoners there and then so that none of them would swim away and escape, but the kind centurion didn't want Paul to die. 'Untie all the prisoners and let them swim ashore!' he ordered. 'Then

ABANDON SHIP!' SPLASH! SPLOOSH! SPLUNSH!
Everyone left the sinking ship. Some crawled, some doggy-paddled and some used pieces of ship as a float, but all 276 passengers, plus Paul, made it safely to dry land.

Fangs for the welcome

They had landed on the island of Malta. The local residents welcomed the dripping refugees very kindly and built a bonfire on the beach to keep them warm. Paul was throwing more kindling on the fire when – 'AAAARRRGH!' he yelled and jerked his arm in the air. A snake that had been hiding among the sticks had slithered out and stuck its fangs into Paul's hand. Everyone could see the viper's zig-zag stripes. But Paul simply shook the snake into the fire and sat down. Everyone looked at him, open-mouthed. What would happen next? Would he swell up, turn black and burst? Would he foam at the mouth and drop dead on the spot? Everyone waited – but nothing happened. *This man is some kind of god!* thought the locals.

Paul and the other passengers were taken to the island's chief, but the chief was distracted because his dad was tossing and turning in bed, fiery with fever and a disgusting tummy disease. Paul went to see him, laid hands on him and said a prayer. SWOOOSH! The fever evaporated like steam and the

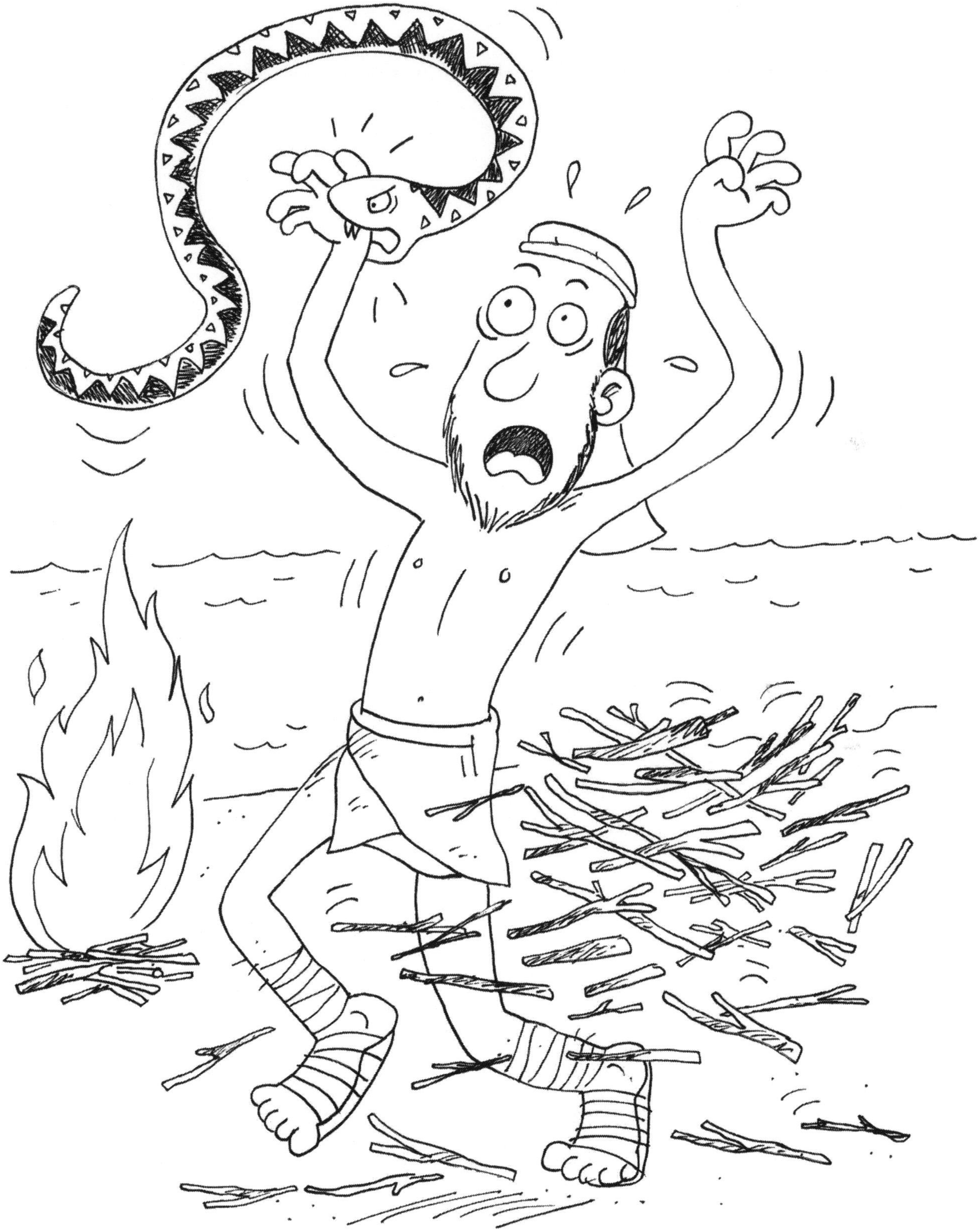

disgusting tummy disease disappeared. This miracle brought every sick person in Malta to the chief's door, so Paul rolled up his sleeves and cured them all.

The road to Rome

Once winter was over and it was safe to sail again, Paul said a fond farewell to Malta and boarded a new ship with his fellow prisoners, their guards and crew. At ports along the way he was cheered by new believers: '**HALLELUJAH! JESUS IS LORD!**' they shouted. At last Paul arrived in Rome, and Jesus-lovers came from far and wide to see him. '**PRAISE THE LORD!**' they yelled.

'**HALLELUJAH!**' cried Paul in reply. Although he was still a prisoner and was going to live under house arrest in Rome, all these new believers made him feel brave.

The first thing Paul did was to summon all the local Jewish leaders to his house. A huge crowd came, and all day long Paul explained everything to them about Jesus, the promised Messiah, and how the Holy Spirit spoke the truth about him through the prophets. Some said, '**YES! I SEE!**' but others said, '**NEVER! I WON'T BELIEVE IT!**' and they argued with each other.

Paul said, 'Is this is how you accept **GOD'S GOOD NEWS?** This is why he's going to share it with the Gentiles, too – at least **THEY** will listen!'

Paul spent the rest of his life sharing the good news, or gospel, *of Jesus, opening up the Church to Jews and non-Jews alike. For the next two years he taught people about Jesus at home where he was under house arrest. We don't know exactly what happened to Paul after this, but he may have been released before he was finally executed by the Romans in AD 65. In spite of his own troubles, Paul kept encouraging new believers, and his letters to the churches in Rome, Corinth and other cities are part of the New Testament. They still encourage and challenge Christians today.*

You can read this story in Acts 27–28.

BEASTLY BONUS STORY

THE END AND THE BEGINNING
John's jaw-dropping dream

Real revelation

Listen to me – I am John the Jesus-lover. I was beaten up and banished to a desert island because of my beliefs, so I was all alone when something blew my mind and boggled my brain: it was the wildest, weirdest and most wonderful vision I have ever had – an unforgettable gift from God. Here's what happened . . .

'**JOOOOOHN!**' The Voice blasted behind me like a trumpet.

I turned round to see who had spoken, and **OH!** There were seven gleaming golden lamps, and in the middle stood someone who looked like the Son of Man:* it was Jesus himself, all dressed in white and gold! His hair and beard were dazzling white, his eyes were fiery and his feet shone! His Voice roared like rivers racing down a mountain! He held seven stars in his hand, and out of his mouth poked a sharp sword! His face blazed brighter than the midday sun!

---

* This is what Jesus called himself. In the Old Testament, 'son of man' can be another way of saying 'human being', but Jesus used it as a title to mean something like 'Son of God' or 'Messiah'.

I fell at his feet but he touched me gently and said, 'Don't be scared! I was dead, but now I am **ALIVE FOR EVER AND EVER!** I am **MORE POWERFUL THAN DEATH ITSELF!**' Then he told me to pay attention and write down everything that happened next . . .

First came seven letters for seven churches, and I wrote down every word. Then the same Voice, as loud as a trumpet, said, '**LOOK AT THIS!**'

WOW! Immediately I was in a trance – and I was in heaven! There was **GOD!** He shone like fiery jewels and was sitting on a throne. A crystal floor spread beneath his feet and an emerald rainbow curved above him. **FIZZZACK! CRAAICK!** Lightning shot from the throne, followed by thunder: **BRROOOAAMMM! BRRROOOOAAAMM!** Behind the throne were people in white, wearing golden crowns, and in front were seven flaming torches – I knew they were the seven spirits of God. But more amazing than the jewels, the fire, the fine folk, the thunder and the lightning were the *creatures* – I'd never seen anything like them! There were four of them: they looked like a lion, a bull, a man and an eagle, but they each had six wings and – weirdest of all – they were covered in eyes, which rolled around and looked in all directions at once! And they never stopped singing:

HOLY, HOLY, HOLY, LORD GOD ALMIGHTY, WHO IS AND WAS AND WILL ALWAYS BE!

Then I saw that God had a scroll which was covered in writing and sealed with seven wax seals. '**WHO CAN BREAK THESE SEALS?**' boomed an awesome angel, but no one could, and that made me very sad.

'**LOOK!**' said one of the fine folk. '**HE CAN!**' Then I saw something very strange: a slaughtered lamb with seven horns and seven eyes! But this wasn't any old lamb – this was Jesus again, the Lamb of God who takes away the sins of the world!* He took the scroll and everyone sang a new song:

BLESSING AND HONOUR AND GLORY AND POWER
BELONG TO THE ONE ON THE THRONE
AND TO THE LAMB
FOR EVER AND EVER!

'**AMEN!**' agreed the creatures covered with eyes, with a roar, a bellow, a shout and a screech.

---

* John the Baptiser compared Jesus to the perfect lamb that Jewish people used to sacrifice in order to get rid of sin. Jesus is still called 'the Lamb of God' in churches today. You can read about the time when John gave Jesus this name in *The Saviour gets a soaking* in **Beastly Bible Stories 3**. You can learn more about animal sacrifice in *Blood and guts* in **Beastly Bible Stories 2**.

Then the Lamb began to open the wax seals on the scroll . . .

Seven seals

Seals numbers one, two, three and four broke open and, **'NEEEEIIIGHH! HHHFNNNH!'** Four riders appeared on four wild, snorting horses. The first came to fight and win: he was Conquest. The second came to destroy peace: he was War. The third came to snatch food from the poor: he was Starvation. The fourth, the most terrible of all, brought fighting and famine, predators and plague: he was Death. The four horsemen rode out into the world.

Seal number five broke open and, **'OH, LOOORD!'** came an unearthly cry. It was a crowd of souls who had been killed for believing in God. 'When will you make things right on earth?' they wailed, but they didn't have much longer to wait, because God was (and is and will always be) in charge.

Seal number six broke open and **BRRROOOOO-AAAGHGHGH!!** Watch out world – a powerful earthquake shook the whole planet. **CRAAAAIISH BRUNNNK!** Buildings everywhere were reduced to rubble, but no one could see because the sun suddenly went black, the moon turned into a puddle of blood and the stars fell from the sky like autumn leaves. **SWWWOOOOSH!** The sky vanished into thin air.

BRRRUUMMMP! Mountains toppled and islands sank without trace. Creation was coming apart at the seams, and everyone on earth – from kings to kitchen slaves – hid in caves and cowered. '**WHOOO WILL SAAAAVE UUUUS?**' they wailed.

An angel came to the rescue and searched the world for God's servants. **WHOOOOSH!** Before I knew what had happened, I was back in heaven with God on his throne and the Lamb by his side, and all around me were uncountable millions of people – different races, different skin colours, different languages, all worshipping God and the Lamb. Everyone joined in with the angels' song:

AMEN!
BLESSING AND GLORY AND WISDOM
AND THANKSGIVING
AND HONOUR AND POWER AND MIGHT
BE TO OUR GOD FOR EVER AND EVER!
AMEN!

Then the Lamb broke open seal number seven and – ' ' Silence! No one said anything at all for about half an hour.

Appalling apocalypse

Then I saw seven awful angels, each with a trumpet. One by one, each trumpet blew: **PAAAAARP! BAM! BAM!** Hail hit the earth and fire and blood rained down. **RROOOORSH!** A wildfire burned up grass and trees everywhere.

PAAAAARP! BRRRUUMMMPSSHH! A fiery mountain hit the sea: the water turned to blood and finished off all the fish.

PAAAAARP! SWAAAZZK! A star fell out of the sky and smacked into the rivers, poisoning the water and everyone who drank it.

PAAAAARP! The sun, moon and stars were next: **CRAICK!** Each lost a third of its light.

PAAAAARP! SWAAAZZK! Another star hit the earth and burst open the Deep Dark! Smoke billowed out along with giant lady-faced locusts with scorpion tails who tortured people wherever they found them.

PAAAAARP! Four fighting angels led an army of 200 million soldiers into war against the world: '**RAAAARGH!**' Their lion-headed horses breathed fire, smoke and poison gas. One third of humankind was killed, while the rest went on murdering, stealing, casting spells, lying and worshipping idols – not one of them said sorry or changed their ways.

PAAAAARP! Finally, the seventh angel blew his trumpet and everyone in heaven shouted, '**THE KINGDOM OF GOD HAS COME! THE WORLD BELONGS TO ALMIGHTY GOD AND HIS MESSIAH!**'

Suddenly – '**RROOOOAAARRGH!**' A great red dragon appeared with seven heads, seven crowns and ten horns! With his terrible tail he swept the stars from the sky: **SWAAAZZK! SWIIIZZK! SWAAAZZK!**

The head of heaven's army was the mighty angel, Michael: he shouted, '**THIS MEANS WAR!**' Michael and his armed angels battled the dragon until they defeated him and threw him out of heaven. He hit the earth – **WHUUUUMP** – but survived. It would take more than a skydive to kill off that Devil of a dragon (also known as the sneaky snake, Satan).*

The dragon had landed on a beach – but what was happening in the sea? I saw a huge and horrible beast rising from the waves! It had a leopard's body, bear's paws and lots of horned heads (including one that looked dead but wasn't), each one with a lion's massive mouth. The dragon gave it power over the whole world, and everyone started worshipping the big beast and the dragon. The big beast was the boss and he said terrible, boastful things. He was

---

* He appeared right back at the beginning of the Bible in *The snake who spoiled everything* and *God vs Satan* in **Beastly Bible Stories 1**.

backed up by his right-hand man, another beast who had lamb's horns and a dragon's roar. This beast made amazing things happen – look! Firebolts from out of the blue! A statue of the big beast that comes to life! This beast branded everyone with his number, to show that they belonged to him: 666.

Then a crowd of angels appeared in front of the big beast's adoring fans. They had a warning for everyone on earth: '**FEAR GOD! WORSHIP HIM! GIVE HIM THE GLORY!** Because it's time for him to **JUDGE YOU ALL!**'

I looked up to heaven and I saw everyone who was safe, singing God's praises. Then I looked back and saw seven angels, one after another, emptying bowls full of plagues onto the earth. The first brought disgusting sores to everyone who had been marked '666'; the second turned the sea to blood and killed all the creatures in it. The third turned the rivers to blood, and the fourth turned up the sun's heat so that everyone's skin was scorched. The fifth blotted out the big beast's throne, and the sixth dried up a mighty river. Finally, the seventh plague battered the earth with storms, shattered cities with earthquakes and hammered people with huge hailstones. '**IT'S DONE!**' said the seventh angel.

Then I saw heaven burst open, and a hero came down on a white horse! His eyes were as fierce as fire, his head sparkled with jewels and a sharp sword came out of his mouth. He was called the Word of God,* and on his armour it said, 'King of kings and Lord of lords' – it was Jesus again! Behind him was heaven's army – uncountable white-robed soldiers on white horses.

* This is what Jesus is called at the beginning of John's Gospel (John 1:1-18).

Heaven's enemies were the dragon, the big beast and the beast's right-hand man, backed up by all the powerful people in the world who worshipped them. An angel shouted, '**LET BATTLE BEGIN!**' **CRUNSSCH! SWLASH! SKWELLUNCH!** The hero's sword killed everyone, and his army captured the beasts. The pair were thrown alive into a lake of fire: **SPLOOONSH! SPLUNSH!** Then – **WHOOOOSH!** – an angel swooped down from heaven, chained up the dragon and chucked him into the Deep Dark for 1000 years. (Later he got out and tried to start a whole new war, but he ended up with the beasts in the lake of fire: **SPLOOONSH!**)

All things new

At last I found myself back where I began: in front of God's shining throne. The old heaven and earth were evaporating, but God was surrounded by everyone who had come back from the dead. He checked the big record books, where everything people had ever done was written down, and he judged them all according to the choices they had made. '**AAAIIIEEEEEEEE!**' Down went all the murderers, thieves, sorcerers, liars and idol worshippers into the lake of fire, along with Death himself.

Then I saw a new heaven and a new earth! And there was a brand-new holy city to replace the old Jerusalem! Here's what I saw: the entire city is made of gold and precious stones and it shines with God's glory! Its gates are always open to anyone in the whole world who loves the Lamb of God. A crystal clear river rushes through the city: it flows from the throne of God and the Lamb, and it's full of the water of life. The Tree of Life grows on its banks and produces fruit all year round. And everywhere people are worshipping God!

I heard a Voice from the throne saying, 'Look! God is coming to live with you, and you will be his people, and he will be your God! It's all over now – there will be no more crying, no more pain, and Death is finished!'

Finally, an angel gave me this message for you from Jesus himself: '**COME!** If you are thirsty, come to me: help yourself to the water of life! I am the A and the Z, the first and the last, the beginning and the end – and I'm coming back soon!'

I, John the Jesus-lover, have truthfully told you everything that I saw and heard in my vision that day, which came from God and his Son, Jesus. Remember what he said: 'I'm coming back soon!'

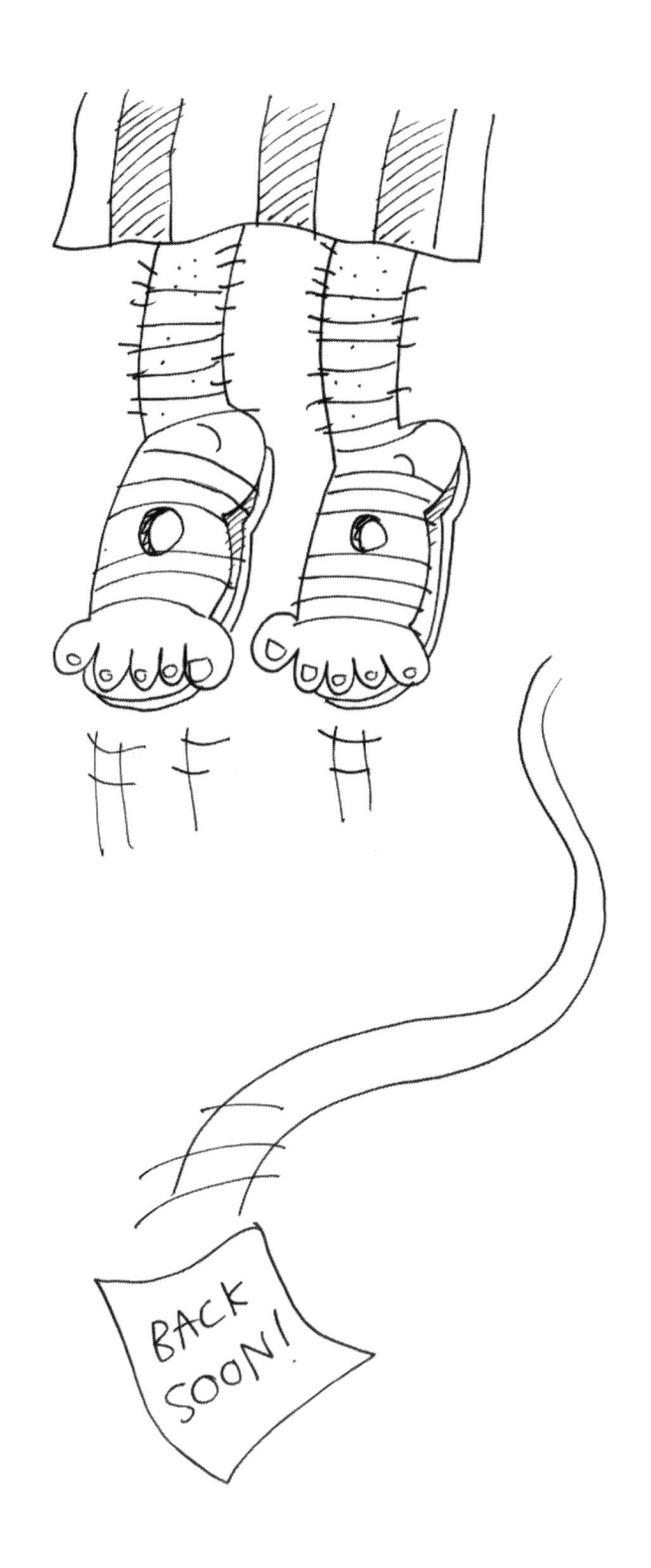

We haven't seen such vivid visions full of weird and wonderful things since the prophets (especially Ezekiel) in **Beastly Bible Stories 1***! However, John's visions don't foretell the future so much as tell the truth about God: they are a kind of 'unveiling', which in Latin is called 'Revelation' and in Greek, 'Apocalypse'. John's amazing dreams showed him how things really are: in spite of all the bad things that happen, God is always totally in charge and he wants all his people (including you and me) to love him and live with him forever.*

You can read about John's visions in the last book of the Bible: Revelation.